THE EXALTATION OF CHRIST JESUS

**Home and Church
Bible Study Commentaries
From**

THE
BOOK
of
HEBREWS

REVISED EDITION

**By
LARRY D. ALEXANDER**

**Plus: "Adherents of the Way, the Truth, and the Life" (A bonus section
on the lives of JESUS' hand-picked apostles, including the Apostle Paul)**

Dedicated in memory of my mother, Janie Juanita Caruthers Alexander
February 8, 1930 – April 2, 2009

CONTENTS

CONTENTS

CONTENTS

INTRODUCTION

Larry D. Alexander is a well-known visual artist, who says he was called by GOD to learn, and to teach GOD's holy word. Alexander has been teaching Sunday school and bible studies for the past seven years, and, has an online weekly Sunday school lesson commentary (http://larrydalexander.blogspot.com/index.html) and also

Sunday school lessons commentary videos on "you tube".

This study of the book of Hebrews follows a trilogy of bible study books written by Alexander in 2006 and early 2007, *(Sunday lessons from the book of the Acts of the Apostles, Sunday school lessons from the Gospel according to John Mark, and Sunday school lessons from the Apostle Paul's letter to the Romans)* which were aimed at helping Christians conform, more fully, to the word of GOD, in their churches, homes, and communities.

The trilogy was followed in 2008 by Alexander's "*Home Bible Study Commentaries from the Gospel of John*", a complete chapter by chapter study guide of the apostle John's account of JESUS' three-year ministry here on earth.

This, latest book, contains Alexander's commentaries from the pages of the letter of Hebrews, the book that exalts the role and person of CHRIST JESUS, perhaps, better than any book in the bible. This study guide is written to promote Christian spiritual growth, as well as to help us to understand JESUS' life, purpose, and superiority over the angels, Moses and all the other prophets, and everything else in all of creation. This, like all of Alexander's books, serves to help develop understanding, fear, and reverence for the ONLY WISE GOD, WHO is our SAVIOR through JESUS CHRIST.

HOW WE GOT OUR BIBLE

Much has been written about how GOD inspired men to write the pages of the bible. GOD used about forty men to write the scriptures and some of these authors remain a mystery even today. The writers of the last chapter of Deuteronomy, the book of Job, and many of the Psalms are classic examples of biblical texts with unknown human authors.

We do not have a single manuscript in the handwriting of Moses, Isaiah, Paul, or any other original writer. That of course always leads to this eternal question, "How do we know that the bible we have today is the written word of those original writers who were inspired by GOD?

We already know that GOD did not inspire all those who copied, or translated the bible into various versions, as HE did the original writers. It is quite evident to those who study to be scholars, that, while the original writers were guided and kept from making mistakes by the power of GOD, both copyists and translators were not, and, could and did make errors.

Even though we have no part of the bible in the handwriting of the original writers, we do have two kinds of sources from which we can learn what the original writers wrote. These sources are called "manuscripts" and "versions". "Manuscripts" are documents written by hand. In the days before printing was invented, this was the only way of producing books. There are no known bible manuscripts that were written by the original authors available to man today. However, we have many copies of manuscripts that were either copied from the original manuscripts, or, from copies of them.

"Versions" are translations of a document into a different language. Some of our ancient versions were actually translated from copies of manuscripts older than any we have today. Therefore, they help us to know exactly what the original writers wrote.

The Old Testament books were written in the Hebrew and Aramaic languages between 1400 and 400 B.C. The oldest bible "manuscript" copies we have today, were the ones found among the now famous "Dead Sea Scrolls" in 1947 and later.
These copies date back to circa 100 B.C.

The oldest known "version" of the Old Testament is the Greek version known as the "Septuagint", which was written by seventy Jewish scholars in Alexandria, Egypt in about 250 B.C., from Hebrew manuscript copies older than any we have today.

In the first half of the second century the bible was translated into Syriac, and not much later, into Latin. A more careful Latin version was completed, around 400

B.C. by the famous scholar, Jerome, called the "Vulgate", which means "common and proper". This version went on to become the official bible of the Roman Catholic Church, and, of Western Europe. Made from very ancient manuscript copies, this book helps us to be sure the bible we have is approximately the same as the original writings.

In 1380 John Wycliffe and his team of scholars translated the bible into "middle English", a blend of "Norman French and Anglo-Saxon languages. This version was translated directly from the Latin Vulgate.

In 1525, William Tyndale wrote an English version, of the New Testament. He later translated some of the Old Testament books into English. His version was translated directly from the original Hebrew and Greek manuscript copies. English churchmen angrily opposed Tyndale's version, and they, along with king Henry VIII, decided instead to go with an English version written by Myles Coverdale. Coverdale used the Latin Vulgate and Martin Luther's German version for his translations.

In Geneva, Switzerland, William Wittington and his group of scholars wrote a revised English version that came to be known as the "Geneva Bible" in 1560. Some of the marginal notes in the Geneva bible offended the Bishops of the Church at England, and this led to the writing of the "Bishops Bible" in 1568. Through the remainder of that century, the Bishop's Bible and the Geneva Bible were split among the churchmen in popularity.

In 1604, however, King James I appointed a commission of 54 scholars, led by Robert Barker, to write a new English version of scriptures. They mostly followed the Bishop's Bible, but they also consulted other English translations, along with the German, Greek and Hebrew text, the Syriac, the Septuagint, and several Latin versions. In 1611 they completed the book and it went on to become the most printed and used text in the history of the English Language, "The King James Version" of the Bible.

However, as the world would have it, all living languages are constantly changing. Many words used in the King James Version are now unknown, or obsolete. Some examples are "nessing", "besom", and "wist". Other words have actually changed their meanings. For example "let", in those days, meant "to hinder" (Romans 1:13). Now, however, it means "to permit". The word "conversation", in those days meant "your whole way of living", but today it just means "talk".

Today, just like in the old days, every Christian needs a bible, translated in their modern native tongue, and in this country that means a "New Living Translation" version of the bible. No translation or version has ever been translated without error, and that includes the "King James Version". And the reason that it has never been done is because there has never been a perfect scholar, or perfect man period, except CHRIST JESUS, and HE didn't choose to write one.

However most of our available versions are good enough to familiarize us with the Word of GOD that has been handed down to us since the foundation of this world. We should trust that GOD is still with us, just as HE was with the original writers, and while we may think or believe that there may be no more inspired writers, I believe more so that GOD still wants us to get to know HIM through HIS word, and the best way we can understand HIS word is in our own modern-day language.

So let's just try and retire the King James Version to our library of reference books, where it can serve us in our studies most efficiently. GOD wants us to get to know HIM and just like in all generations before us, HE raises up scholars to interpret HIS word in our own present-day language.

Larry D. Alexander

UNDERSTANDING WHO JESUS IS

SCRIPTURE REVEALS FOUR IMPORTANT ASPECTS OF CHRIST' PERSON:

1.   The seven positions of CHRIST

2.   CHRIST'S offices

3   CHRISTS' SONship

4   The Hypostatic Union

THE SEVEN POSITIONS OF CHRIST

- Pre-incarnate – possessed all the glory and attributes of GOD the FATHER, except HE was not all-knowing at this point, only GOD the FATHER was. (Genesis 22:11-17) (Matthew 24:36)
- Incarnate – Displayed perfect humanity as a 100% human, and HIS deity remained undiminished. Still not all-knowing at this point (Matthew 24:36) (Mark 2:10) (John 5:16-30) (John 17:2)
- In death – JESUS revealed GOD's love, righteousness, wisdom, and method of making possible the redemption on mankind.
- In resurrection – JESUS revealed the power of GOD, and GOD's plan to glorify humanity. Gained all power on earth and in Heaven at this point and is now equal with GOD in every aspect, including all-knowing. (Matthew 28:18)
- In ascension – JESUS ascended back into Heaven and is now seated on HIS throne serving as head of the Christian Body of Believers. HE is now omnipresent in all who choose to believe, worship and follow HIM.
- The Rapture (seen only by the Church) – (Matthew 24) (1 Thessalonians 4:13-17)

- The Second Coming (seen by the world) – The Millennial Kingdom (Revelation 20:1-6) (Matthew 24) (Matthew 25:31-46)

JESUS' OFFICES

The title "CHRIST" in the New Testament, as well as the title "MESSIAH" in the Old Testament imply a "threefold" official divine responsibility or function. They are;

- Prophet
- Priest
- King

JESUS is the only person in Scripture WHOSE ministry involves all three of these offices.

AS PROPHET

In the biblical Greek, the word used for "messenger" is "Angelos", and it describes one who brings news or tidings by divine order from GOD. JESUS came to usher in a "New Covenant" from GOD. It is a Covenant that is far superior to any before or since that time. The message of the "Good News" or "Gospel" that was announced by John the Baptist and ushered in by JESUS is the greatest and most important fulfilled prophecy of all time.

In the Old Testament, prophets were reformers of sort, who, not only delivered GOD's Word, but also, at one and the same time, challenged the people to actually serve the LORD and obey HIS Word. They were called "men of GOD" or "seers", and were distinguished by their holy lifestyle before men, under GOD. They were able to see beyond that which is natural in the eyes of man.

JESUS wholly fitted the role of the Old Testament prophet. In fact, in the Old Testament, JESUS served in the role of a prophet as "The ANGEL of GOD" and "The COMMANDER of the LORD's Army" (Joshua 5:13-15) delivering many messages from GOD the FATHER to men such as Abraham (Genesis 22:11-17), Moses (Exodus 3:2-3), Joshua (Joshua 5:13-15), Baalam (Numbers 22:21-35), and to the Israelites in general at Bokim (Judges 2:1-5).

AS PRIEST

JESUS completely filled the office of priest, as it is described in the Old Testament, and as it is taught in the New Testament, in the book of Hebrews (Hebrews 7:1-14). HE fulfilled the "Aaronic Priesthood" type, as one who offers up gifts and sacrifices, and as an interceder for the LORD's people. JESUS' priesthood is also compared to that of Melchizedek, the historical, obscure figure to whom even Abraham paid tithes (Genesis 15:17-20).

JESUS, like Melchizedek, is a King/Priest. As King/Priest, JESUS heads the Christian Church, which make it a holy and royal priesthood (1 Peter 2:5 & 9). And so, the Christian Church is a Priesthood, whereby every believer is a priest. And the fact that the Church itself is a Priesthood, makes CHRIST JESUS, WHO is the head of the Church, our High Priest.

JESUS received priesthood by divine appointment from GOD. Like Melchizedek, HE did not derive HIS priesthood from HIS lineage, and there are no descending priests who succeeded HIM. As priests under CHRIST, Christians must offer a fivefold sacrifice:

- Their own bodies (Romans 12:1, Philippians 2:17, 2 Timothy 4:6, James 1:27)
- Praise to GOD (Hebrews 13:15)
- The sacrifice of good works (Hebrews 13:15)
- Sharing gifts of money and service to those in need (Romans 12:13, Galatians 6:6, & 10, Titus 3:14)
- Be intercessors in prayer for others (Colossians 4:12, 1 Timothy 2:1)

AS KING:

JESUS fulfills the office of King as it is foretold in the "Davidic Covenant" (2 Samuel 7:11-13). Also see Isaiah 9:6-7, Luke 1:31-33. Scripture tells that JESUS will come again, not just as "King of the Jews", but rather, as "LORD of all Kings" (Revelations 19:6). Recognition of JESUS' three offices is paramount to Christian Theology and Faith, for they not only describe HIS person, but also HIS work in the three spheres that man must travel through, the past, the present, and, the future.

JESUS' SONSHIPS

In the bible JESUS is presented as having four son-ships while HE was here on earth: HE was known as the <u>SON of GOD</u>, <u>SON of man</u>, <u>SON of David</u>, <u>SON of Abraham</u>, and <u>SON of Mary</u>:

SON OF GOD

In the biblical Greek, the word used for "only begotten" is "monogenes" and it is used five times in the Gospel of John to reference, just WHO JESUS is. GOD is eternally the FATHER of CHRIST JESUS, and CHRIST JESUS is eternally the SON of GOD. The TRINITY (GOD the FATHER, GOD the SON, and GOD the HOLY SPIRIT) is quite literally the "ETERNAL GENERATION", and this terminology lends reason to the fact, that, even though it is not "generation" in the ordinary sense of the word, THEIR generation is unique and eternal because there is no beginning or end to it, and, there was never a time when it did not exist (Isaiah 9:6, John 1:1-18 & 3:16-17, Galatians 4:4).

SON OF MAN

CHRIST is called "The SON of Man" 80 times in the New Testament. It is a term that speaks to the "humanity of JESUS, and signifies that HE represented "the human race" in what HE did here on earth. In fact, HE spent HIS first thirty years on earth, showing us how to live perfectly as human beings under GOD.

In the Old Testament the term "son of man" is used in the Book of Ezekiel 90 times by the LORD to address the prophet Ezekiel, who HE used to represent the concept of a "coming MAN" from Heaven, WHO would be blessed by GOD (JESUS). Failure to emphasize and declare the humanity of JESUS is just as destructive to Christian doctrine as denying HIS deity, and is indeed, a sign of a "false prophet", or antichrist (1 John 4:1-3).

SON OF DAVID

JESUS is the ONE WHO the bible says will reign on the throne of David forever (2 Samuel 7:11-13, Matthew 1:1, 6, 20, 9:27, 12:23, 15:22, 20:30-31, 21:9). JESUS is also seen as a descendant of David in Revelations 3:7, 5:5, and 22:16. The fact that JESUS is called the SON of David tells us that GOD's plan was for HIM to fulfill the covenant promise that HE had given to David when HE said that one of his descendants would always sit on his throne in Israel.

SON OF ABRAHAM

The "Abrahamic Covenant", the "Davidic Covenant", and the Covenant ushered in by JESUS are all linked together and serve to give CHRIST an inseparable role in the eternal promise of GOD's blessings upon mankind. The title "SON of Abraham", like the "SON of David" relates JESUS to the promise given to Abraham by GOD (Matthew 1:1, Luke 3:23-34, & 19:9).

The promise to David links JESUS to the throne of Israel, while the promise to Abraham links JESUS extensively to the entire human race (Genesis 12:3). It indicates the wide extent of JESUS' ministry, and also forms the basis for the Gospel to be preached throughout the world (Matthew 28:18-20).

SON OF MARY

Another title given to JESUS is that HE is the "SON of Mary" (Luke 1:26-38, 2:1-7, Matthew 13:55). In order for JESUS to be presented as a perfect sacrifice for the sins of man, HE had to be, first, born of woman so that HE could operate here on earth as a 100% human being.

GOD's requirement as payment for sin has always been in the form of a perfect, unblemished sacrifice. Mary was the woman chosen by GOD, through which HE would deliver JESUS to mankind as an propitiation for our sins, once and for all time. HE lived HIS first thirty years or so on earth specifically to show us how to live and operate perfectly under GOD, without the embodiment of the HOLY SPIRIT.

Remember, the HOLY SPIRIT did not come upon JESUS until HE was approximately thirty years old, after HIS baptism by John (Matthew 3:16, Mark 1:10, Luke 3:21-22, John 1:29-34), and HE had lived perfectly under GOD even up to that point, because HE shared "GOD's nature" just as all human beings do, who, do not live perfectly under GOD. And so the absence of the HOLY SPIRIT in man can no longer be used as an excuse to sin.

THE HYPOSTATIC UNION

The uniqueness of the person of CHRIST includes all that GOD is, and all that man is, apart from sin. In our understanding of Scripture as it pertains to the incarnate CHRIST, one must be extremely careful not to neglect all the evidence of HIS deity, or, the essential character of HIS humanity. And while it may be difficult to detect exactly how these two natures meld in their work and activities, it is only necessary that we understand that the embodiment of the two natures constitute history's one and only "Theanthropic Person". No one, before or after CHRIST, will ever possess both these characteristics. JESUS was both 100% man, and, 100% GOD.

INTRODUCTION TO THE LETTER OF HEBREWS

The book of Hebrews was written to address the issues that those Jewish believers had in making the transition from the Old Testament Levitical system to their newfound freedom in CHRIST JESUS. This book describes in great detail, the superiority of CHRIST to everything in the Old Testament, including the entire priesthood, and, the old animal and plant sacrificial system.

This letter we call Hebrews, is the only epistle in the New Testament that does not begin like a first-century letter. There is no opening salutation, or prayer, and, because neither the writer, nor the addressee are identified in the opening lines, there has been a polemical assault waged upon this invaluable Christian document for quite some time.

For a long time this letter was attributed to the apostle Paul, however, more recent scholars have all but disproved the likelihood of him being the author. This is primarily because the Greek style of the book of Hebrews is so greatly different from any of Paul's other writings. Martin Luther argued that Apollos, a disciple of John the Baptist, was the author, while other scholars have advanced authorship to Priscilla, who, along with her husband, Aquila, was a pioneer in the "House Church" concept that became very popular shortly after the ascension of CHRIST in the early first century.

But perhaps the most compelling argument for authorship favors Barnabas, who was known as "The Enabling Encourager". Barnabas is the man, who Scriptures say, first introduced the Apostle Paul to the Church, when he did so, first, to the apostles at Jerusalem in Acts chapter 9, and then later on, to the church at Antioch of Syria, in Acts chapter 11. In fact, Barnabas even traveled for a year with Paul, during Paul's first missionary journey, but later, fell out with him, over differences involving John Mark, Barnabas' cousin, and the eventual author of the book of Mark.

Tertullian, the great church scholar, Jerome, the author of the Vulgate (the first Latin translation of the Bible), Gregory of Elvira, and Filaster (fourth century writers), all share the opinion that Barnabas is the author. In fact, they all refer to the book of Hebrews as "an epistle by Barnabas". But no matter who wrote this invaluable Christian document, it is certain that the author had in-depth knowledge of the Old Testament, particularly the Pentateuch (the first five books of the bible), and also, the Psalms. The writer of this letter also had a distinctively clear understanding of the perspective that was provided by CHRIST JESUS, during HIS three-year ministry.

The letter of Hebrews, perhaps more than any other writing in scripture, highly exalts the person and works of our LORD and SAVIOR, JESUS CHRIST. It makes valuable contributions to the doctrinal aspects of JESUS' priesthood, incarnation, and vicarious sacrifice. It also goes a long ways toward developing an understanding, regarding the relationship between the interpretation of Old Testament Law, and New Testament Faith. It also helps us to understand the "New Covenant" that was ushered in by CHRIST, as it relates to the "Old Covenant" that was given to Moses, by GOD, on Mount Sinai.

CHAPTER ONE:

JESUS CHRIST IS GOD'S SON

SCRIPTURE:
The King James Version
Hebrews 1:1-3

1 (1) GOD, WHO at sundry times and in divers manners spake in time past unto the fathers by the prophets, (2) Hath in these last days spoken unto us by HIS SON, WHOM HE hath appointed HEIR of all things, by WHOM also HE made the worlds; (3) WHO being the brightness of HIS glory, and the express image of HIS person, and upholding all things by the word of HIS power, when HE had by HIMSELF purged our sins, sat down on the right hand of the MAJESTY ON HIGH;

COMMENTARY:

Long ago, GOD spoke "many times and in many different ways" (polymeros kai polytropos) to our ancestors, through the prophets. However, today, GOD continuously speaks to us through HIS SON, JESUS CHRIST, WHO is "The Word".

"Prototokas" is the word that is used here in chapter 1, verse 2, and later, in verse 6, for the term "SON" in the original Greek writing. Throughout the New Testament, it is a word that is only used in reference to JESUS HIMSELF, and it means, quite simply, "FIRSTBORN". It is a technical theological term that affirms HIS supreme rank and unique relationship and position in the family of GOD. That is why, even the angels of GOD, worship the SON.

The "right hand" is the traditional place of power and authority in the biblical sense, and so JESUS not only possesses eternal life and existence, by being at the right hand of GOD the FATHER in Heaven, HE also exercises all of the power and authority of Deity. As FIRSTBORN, GOD promised everything to the SON as an inheritance, and through HIM, HE made the universe and everything in it.

In the New Testament Greek, the word used for "brightness" is "apaugasma" (apow-gas-mah), and it is a "brilliance", "effulgence", or "light", which is reflected from one place, or object, to another place or object". JESUS is the "LIGHT" that wants to shine on all mankind, and gives each of us that light, so that we too, can shine that light on someone else, making them able to see their way through the darkness that presses to dominate this world. And so, here in Hebrews 1:3, that is the word that is being used by the author to describe JESUS CHRIST in his original Greek rendering.

Also in verse three, the author uses another interesting Greek term to depict JESUS. That term is "charakter" (khar-ak-tare), and it means "express image". It is from that word that we derive our English word "character". It is "an exact copy, or representation of", and, it is like a seal, an impression, or stamp. Here the author attempts to establish the person of JESUS CHRIST as being superior to any other prophet, or intermediary that GOD had sent prior to HIS coming. He also sought to affirm that JESUS is truly "the SON of the living GOD", and, is the "exact image" of GOD HIMSELF. And so, in JESUS, and through HIS behavior, we are able to see exactly what GOD is like.

JESUS IS GREATER THAN THE ANGELS
Hebrews 1:4-14

1 (4) Being made so much better than the angels, as HE hath by inheritance obtained a more excellent name than they. (5) For unto which of the angels said HE at any time, "THOU art MY SON, this day I have begotten THEE?" And again, "I will be to HIM a FATHER, and HE shall be to ME a SON?" (6) And again, when HE bringeth in the FIRSTBEGOTTEN into the world, HE saith, "And let all the angels of GOD worship HIM". (7) And of the angels HE saith, "WHO maketh HIS angels spirits, and HIS ministers a flame of fire". (8) But unto the SON HE saith, "THY throne, O GOD, is for ever and ever: a scepter of righteousness is the scepter of THY kingdom". (9) "THOU hast loved righteousness, and hated iniquity; therefore GOD, even THY GOD, hath anointed THEE with oil of gladness above THY fellows". (10) And, THOU, LORD, in the beginning hast laid the foundation of the earth; and the heavens are the works of THINE hands:" (11) "They shall perish; but THOU remainest; and they all shall wax old as doth a garment; (12) And as a vesture shalt THOU fold them up, and they shall be changed: but THOU art the same, and THY years shall not fail". (13) But to which of the angels said HE at any time, "Sit on MY right hand, until I make THINE enemies THY footstool?" (14) Are they not all ministering spirits, sent forth to minister for them who shall be heirs of salvation?"

COMMENTARY:

In Hebrews 1:4-14, the writer turns his efforts toward proving that JESUS is also superior to angels. In verse 4, he says, in effect, that, JESUS' superior name serves to add to HIS credentials. In biblical times, a person's name often summed up who they were. The name "JESUS" means "JEHOVAH is salvation", and thereby, the very term "SAVIOR" makes HIM eternally superior to any angel, just simply by way of HIS more excellent name.

Verses 13 and 14 serve to remind us of the most important reason why angels should not be the focus of our worship. And that reason being, is that angels are only servants of GOD. Most of them are spirits sent from GOD to care for those who will eventually receive salvation. I say "most of them", because satan also commands a host of angels. We are told of this fact in both Matthew 25:41, and Jude 1:6. Therefore, it is JESUS, not angels, WHO should always be the focus of our Faith.

In the final analysis, the true meaning of life is contained in the person of CHRIST JESUS. HE is our "direct access" to GOD the FATHER. However, we must listen closely for the meaning of the truth we have heard about HIM, lest we be in danger of drifting away from the ALMIGHTY GOD HIMSELF.

If GOD is able to spin the Universe into orbit, tell the sun where to rise, and the oceans where to stop, then certainly, HE can satisfy our quest for the meaning of our existence, direct our path through this life, and, at one and the same, save our souls and secure us for all eternity through CHRIST JESUS.

WHAT DID WE LEARN FROM CHAPTER ONE?
Here are some key points to remember

(1). Through JESUS, GOD made the universe and everything in it. (Hebrews 1:2)

(2). JESUS reflects GOD's OWN image, exactly, and, HE represents GOD exactly. (Hebrews 1:3)

(3). JESUS is far greater than the angels in Heaven, and HIS name is far greater than their names. (Hebrews 1:4)

(4). Like GOD the FATHER, JESUS' nature is immutable, or, unchangeable. (Hebrews 1:8-12)

CHAPTER TWO:

A WARNING AGAINST DRIFTING AWAY

SCRIPTURE:
The King James Version
Hebrews 2:1-4

2 (1) Therefore we ought to give the more earnest heed to the things which we have heard, lest at any time we should let them slip. (2) For if the word spoken by angels was steadfast, and every transgression and disobedience received a just recompence of reward; (3) How shall we escape, if we neglect so great salvation; which at the first began to be spoken by the LORD, and was confirmed unto us by them that heard HIM; (4) GOD also bearing them witness, both with signs and wonders, and with divers miracles, and gifts of the HOLY GHOST, according to HIS OWN will?

COMMENTARY:

In Hebrews chapter 2, verses 1-4, the writer of Hebrews pauses momentarily to give us the first of five warnings that are contained in this letter. The others are in chapters 3-4, 5:11-6:20, 10:19-39, and chapter 12. The warning here in chapter 2 is the most terse of the five, and, is a stern warning against the spiritual immaturity and inertia that the Jews had apparently taken on. It was an attempt by the author to "nip in the bud", any such shortfalls by the new Christian followers. The words of King Solomon may have been ringing in his head, as they are contained in Proverbs 3:21, where it warns, "My son, do not slip away, but keep my counsel and intent".

In the Septuagint Greek rendering of Proverbs 3:21, the same Greek word, "pararrhueo" (par-ar-hroo-eh-o), which means, "drift away", that is used there, is used here in Hebrews 2:1. It means "to let carelessly flow by, or slip away". Here the author is not just speaking to Christians, but rather, he is speaking to anyone who has heard the word of GOD, concerning the great gift of salvation, and chose to ignore it.

This warning must have also certainly impacted those believers of the old religious system of Judaism, as well as it did the new Christians, particularly those Christians who were considering a return back to Judaism. For the converted Jews, turning back to the old system would require them to neglect their newfound salvation in CHRIST JESUS.

The Dead Sea Scrolls, which were discovered in 1947, give us a glimpse of how the early church had been infiltrated with the false teaching of "angel worship" and "angel domination" in the coming age. The Dead Sea scrolls show that the sectarians of Kirbeth-Qumran believed that the coming age would be marked by the domination of the archangel Michael and his angelic subordinates.

Here in this passage, particularly in verses 5-9, the writer of this letter issues a powerful refute to this point of view. Here he lets us know quite clearly, and quite frankly in verse 5 that the future world will not be controlled by angels, but rather, will be controlled by CHRIST JESUS, WHO was made lower than the angels for a little while, and is now crowned with glory and honor, because HE suffered death for us on a cross at Golgotha. As a result, GOD gave HIM authority over all things, and HE is exalted over all creation.

In the author's argument, he quotes from Psalm 8:4-6 and notes that the realm of humanity had been below that of the angels, despite the fact that GOD had given man HIS OWN spiritual image, and dominion. JESUS, WHO voluntarily became one of us, tasted death for everyone in the world. And it is only fitting that GOD, WHO made all things, would bring all HIS children into glory higher than the angels, through the suffering of JESUS CHRIST, HIS SON and our SAVIOR.

In doing this, GOD presents JESUS as a perfect leader (in the Greek, "ACHEGOS"), for HIS people. In other words, JESUS is the PIONEER, ORIGINATOR, and CAPTAIN of our salvation. And so now, JESUS makes holy, all those who choose HIM, and, as a result, GOD becomes their FATHER also. JESUS is not ashamed to call those who choose HIM, HIS brothers and sisters, and, HE proclaims the wonder of GOD's name to each of us in GOD's presence.

Only as a human born to die, could JESUS break the power of sin and death that was held by satan over mankind. It was the only way that HE could deliver us, who were slaves to sin, and the fear of dying. JESUS did not come as an angel because HE did not come to help the angels. HE came as a man, so that HE could be our merciful and faithful HIGH PRIEST before GOD. Only then, could HE offer HIMSELF as a supreme sacrifice that would take away the sins of the world, once and for all time.

JESUS THE MAN
Hebrews 2:5-18

2 (5) For unto the angels hath HE not put in subjection the world to come, whereof we speak. (6) But one in a certain place testified, saying, "What is man, that THOU art mindful of him? Or the son of man that THOU visitest him? (7) THOU madest him a little lower than the angels; THOU crownedst him with glory and honour, and didst set him over the works of THY hands: (8) THOU hast put all things in subjection under his feet". For in that HE put all in subjection under him, HE left nothing that is not put under him. But now we see not yet all things put under him. (9) But we see JESUS, WHO was made a little lower than the angels for the suffering of death, crowned with glory and honour; that HE by the grace of GOD should taste death for every man. (10) For it became HIM, for WHOM are all things, in bringing many sons unto glory, to make the CAPTAIN of their salvation perfect through sufferings. (11) For both HE that sanctifieth and they who are sanctified are all of one: for which cause HE is not ashamed to call them brethren. (12) Saying, "I will declare THY name unto my brethren, in the midst of the church will I sing praise unto THEE". (13) And again, "I will put my trust in HIM". And again, "Behold I and the children which GOD hath given ME". (14) Forasmuch then as the children are partakers of flesh and blood, HE also HIMSELF likewise took part of the same; that through death HE might destroy him that had the power of death, that is, the devil; (15) And deliver them who through fear of death were all their lifetime subject to bondage. (16) For verily HE took not on HIM the nature of angels; but HE took on HIM the seed of Abraham. (17) Wherefore in all things it behoved HIM to be made like unto HIS brethren, that HE might be merciful and faithful HIGH PRIEST in things pertaining to GOD, to make reconciliation for the sins of people. (18) For in that HE HIMSELF hath suffered being tempted, HE is able to succour them that are tempted.

COMMENTARY:

The Dead Sea Scrolls, which were discovered in 1947, give us a glimpse of how the early church had been infiltrated with the false teaching of "angel worship" and "angel domination" in the coming age. The Dead Sea scrolls show that the sectarians of Kirbeth-Qumran believed that the coming age would be marked by the domination of the archangel Michael and his angelic subordinates.

Here in this passage, particularly in verses 5-9, the writer of this letter issues a powerful refute to this point of view. Here he lets us know quite clearly, and quite frankly in verse 5 that the future world will not be controlled by angels, but rather, will be controlled by CHRIST JESUS, WHO was made lower than the angels for a little while, and is now crowned with glory and honor, because HE suffered death for us on a cross at Golgotha. As a result, GOD gave HIM authority over all things, and HE is exalted over all creation.

In the author's argument, he quotes from Psalm 8:4-6 and notes that the realm of humanity had been below that of the angels, despite the fact that GOD had given man HIS OWN spiritual image, and dominion. JESUS, WHO voluntarily became one of us, tasted death for everyone in the world. And it is only fitting that GOD, WHO made all things, would bring all HIS children into glory higher than the angels, through the suffering of JESUS CHRIST, HIS SON and our SAVIOR.

In doing this, GOD presents JESUS as a perfect leader (in the Greek, "ACHEGOS"), for HIS people. In other words, JESUS is the PIONEER, ORIGINATOR, and CAPTAIN of our salvation. And so now, JESUS makes holy, all those who choose HIM, and, as a result, GOD becomes their FATHER also. JESUS is not ashamed to call those who choose HIM, HIS brothers and sisters, and, HE proclaims the wonder of GOD's name to each of us in GOD's presence.

Only as a human born to die, could JESUS break the power of sin and death that was held by satan over mankind. It was the only way that HE could deliver us, who were slaves to sin, and the fear of dying. JESUS did not come as an angel because HE did not come to help the angels. HE came as a man, so that HE could be our merciful and faithful HIGH PRIEST before GOD. Only then, could HE offer HIMSELF as a supreme sacrifice that would take away the sins of the world, once and for all time.

WHAT DID WE LEARN FROM CHAPTER TWO?
Here are some key points to remember

(1). We must study the word of GOD very closely, so that we may not easily drift away from HIS will for our lives. (Hebrews 2:1-4)

(2). In order to save us from condemnation, GOD temporarily made JESUS to be lower than the angels. HE also did this so that ultimately, HE could elevate man, whom HE made in HIS OWN image, to a status higher than the angels. GOD then gave JESUS authority over all things. (Hebrews 2:6-8)

(3). By GOD's grace, JESUS tasted death for everyone in the world. (Hebrews 2:9b)

(4). The only way JESUS could die was by becoming a human being first, and only by dying, could HE break the power that satan had, through death.

CHAPTER THREE:

JESUS IS GREATER THAN MOSES

SCRIPTURE:
The King James Version
Hebrews 3

3 (1) Wherefore, holy brethren, partakers of the heavenly calling, consider the APOSTLE and HIGH PRIEST of our profession, CHRIST JESUS; (2) WHO was faithful to HIM that appointed HIM, as also Moses was faithful in all his house. (3) For this MAN was counted worthy of more glory than Moses, inasmuch as he who hath builded the house hath more honour than the house. (4) For every house is builded by some man; but HE that built all things is GOD. (5) And Moses verily was faithful in all his house, as a servant, for a testimony of those things which were to be spoken after; (6) But CHRIST as a SON over HIS OWN house; WHOSE house are we, if we hold fast the confidence and the rejoicing of the hope firm unto the end. (7) Wherefore (as the HOLY GHOST saith, "To day if ye will hear HIS voice, (8) Harden not your hearts, as in the provocation, in the day of temptation in the wilderness: (9) When your fathers tempted ME, proved ME, and saw MY works forty years. (10) Wherefore I was grieved with that generation, and said, "They do always err in their heart; and they have not known MY ways. (11) So I sware in MY wrath, they shall not enter into MY rest.)" (12) Take heed, brethren, lest there be in any of you an evil heart of unbelief, in departing from the living GOD. (13) But exhort one another daily, while it is called today; lest any of you be hardened through the deceitfulness of sin. (14) For we are made partakers of CHRIST, if we hold the beginning of our confidence steadfast unto the end; (15) While it is said, "Today if ye will hear HIS voice, harden not your hearts, as the provocation, (16) For some, when they had heard, did provoke: howbeit not all that came out of Egypt by Moses. (17) But with some was he grieved forty years? Was it not with them that had sinned, whose carcases fell in the wilderness? (18) And to whom sware HE that they should not enter into HIS rest, but to them that believed not? (19) So we see that they could not enter in because of unbelief.

(10)

COMMENTARY:

The builder of the house is always greater than the house itself. In Hebrews chapter three, the author of GOD turns his focus to proving that JESUS is greater than GOD's great servant Moses, who led the Israelites out of Egypt, during the great exodus. It is a call for faithfulness among the chosen people of GOD, as the writer now addresses his readers as "holy brothers" who share in the Heavenly calling. Here, the author is obviously thinking of the privilege of their own high calling of being able to participate in the future dominion of CHRIST JESUS in HIS coming earthly "Millennial Kingdom".

In this passage, Moses is praised for his faithfulness as an honored servant, who was himself, high above the status of a slave. But he points out that JESUS too, was a faithful servant of HIS FATHER GOD, and was far superior to Moses in every respect. In relationship to GOD's household, Moses was never more than a member of the family. However, JESUS is the architect, or builder of the family of GOD. HE deserves far more glory than Moses, just as a person who builds a house deserves more praise than the house itself.

As far as roles in the house of GOD are concerned Moses was an important servant, however, JESUS is the SON and HEIR of the OWNER of the house, GOD. And even in relationship to ministry, Moses himself spoke of what would happen in the future, when he prophesied in Deuteronomy 18:15, to his fellow Israelites, that, "The LORD will raise up for you a prophet like me from among your fellow Israelites, and you must listen to that PROPHET". In every way imaginable, JESUS was superior to Moses, who was a towering figure in Jewish history, and in fact, is greater than any other human being who has ever lived.

GOD's voice is represented by any of the directives that are given to us through the Holy Scriptures, and, through the HOLY SPIRIT WHO is at work in all believers. True believers will always hear, recognize, and seek to obey that voice. The word "today" in verse 7, reminds us that GOD's voice has a current expression, and we can know HIS will, and hear HIM speak to us, right now, in this current day and time, through HIS Holy Word, and SPIRIT.

The key to our personal relationship with GOD is to remain steadfast and sensitive to HIS HOLY SPIRIT, and always be ready to respond in the right way when HE does speak to us. We must take care that we do not find ourselves in the position of the Israelites, who were made, by GOD, to wander in the desert for forty years, and never was able to experience GOD's "rest" in the new "promised land" of milk and honey, because they disobeyed HIM. In the same way, if we disobey and move against GOD's will today, we ourselves will never experience GOD's rest, which HE has had specially prepared for us in Heaven, from the foundation of this world.

For whosoever the book of Hebrews was originally intended, it is truly a treasure for modern-day Christians as well. It helps us to somehow sense the intimate bond between Old Testament faith, and our own faith in CHRIST JESUS. It also helps us to appreciate just how great of a salvation we have in GOD, through HIS greater SON. GOD's promise of salvation, or, entering into "HIS place of rest", is still valid, and should make us tremble with fear for those who might fail to reach it at the end of this earthly struggle.

WHAT DID WE LEARN FROM CHAPTER THREE?
Here are some key points to remember

(1). GOD is the builder of the house, and the builder of the house is always greater than the house itself. (Hebrews 3:3-4)

(2). JESUS is greater than Moses, who himself, was a great servant of GOD. (Hebrews 3:5-6)

(3). Those who rebel against GOD, will never enter into the Kingdom of Heaven, which is GOD's promised place of rest. (Hebrews 3:16-18)

CHAPTER FOUR:

(12)

THE PROMISED REST FOR GOD'S PEOPLE

SCRIPTURE:
The King James Version
Hebrews 4:1-13

4 (1) Let us therefore fear, lest, a promise being left us of entering into HIS rest, any of you should seem to come short of it. (2) For unto us was the gospel preached, as well as unto them: but the word preached did not profit them, not being mixed with faith in them that heard it. (3) For we which have believed do enter into rest, as HE said, "As I have sworn in MY wrath, if they shall enter into MY rest:" although the works were finished from the foundation of the world. (4) For HE spake in a certain place of the seventh day on this wise, and GOD did rest the seventh day from all HIS works. (5) And in this place again, "If they shall enter into MY rest". (6) Seeing therefore it remaineth that some must enter therein, and they to whom it was first preached entered not in because of unbelief: (7) Again, HE limiteth a certain day, saying David, "To day, after so long a time; as it is said, "Today if ye will hear HIS voice, harden not your hearts". (8) For if JESUS had given them rest, then would HE not afterward have spoken of another day. (9) There remaineth therefore a rest to the people of GOD. (10) For he that is entered into HIS rest, he also has ceased from his own works, as GOD did from HIS. (11) Let us labour therefore to enter into that rest, lest any man fall after the same example of unbelief. (12) For the word of GOD is quick, and powerful, and sharper than any two-edged sword, piercing even to the dividing asunder of the soul and spirit, and of the joints and marrow, and is a discerner of the thoughts and intents of the heart. (13) Neither is there any creature that is not manifest in HIS sight: but all things are naked and opened unto the eyes of HIM with WHOM we have to do.

COMMENTARY:

In chapter 4, the writer of Hebrews continues his discussion of "rest" that he began in chapter 3. He reminds us that GOD's Word has already come. It has, in fact, been with us since the beginning. It came to us just as it did to those in Moses' time with a similar promise of rest to those who choose to hear and respond by faith. The very concept of "GOD's rest" is rooted in creation itself, and, even today, still has vital meaning for believers.

We, as Christians, know of GOD's place of rest, because scripture tells us that on the seventh day, GOD rested from all of HIS labor. And so we see GOD's place of rest, is just like HIS word, and it has always been there for us to enjoy following our earthly experience. And even though many have failed to make it to that place of rest over the generations, it still remains to be enjoyed by those who listen to, and obey CHRIST JESUS.

This place of rest is not like the land of Canaan, where Joshua led the people, following their struggles on the desert all those years ago. God has spoken since that time about another place of rest that is still waiting for those who believe, in this day and time. We will find rest from all of our labors, just as GOD rested after creating the world. But anyone who disobeys GOD in this day, as the Israelite people did, who died in the desert long ago, will also experience a death that will eternally separate them from GOD.

The Word of GOD is full of living power. It cuts deep into our innermost thoughts and desires like the sharpest of two-edged swords. All things lay naked before GOD. HE sees all, hears all, and knows all that we do. And every one of us will have to make an account for the deeds done in our lifetimes. And weather, or not, we believe that HE exists, therefore, becomes totally irrelevant.

JESUS IS OUR HIGH PRIEST
Hebrews 4:14-5:10

4 (14) Seeing then that we have a great HIGH PRIEST, that is passed into the Heavens, JESUS the SON of GOD, let us hold fast our profession. (15) For we have not an high priest which cannot be touched with the feeling of our infirmities; but was in all points tempted like as we are, yet without sin. (16) Let us therefore come boldly unto the throne of grace, that we may obtain mercy, and find grace to help in time of need.

CHAPTER FIVE:

JESUS IS OUR HIGH PRIEST (continued from chapter 4)

SCRIPTURE:
The King James Version
Hebrews 5:1-10

5 (1) For every high priest taken from among men is ordained for men in things pertaining to GOD, that he may offer both gifts and sacrifices for sins: (2) Who can have compassion on the ignorant, and on them that are out of the way; for that he himself also is compassed with infirmity. (3) And by reason hereof he ought, as for people, so also for himself, to offer for sins. (4) And no man taketh this honour unto himself, but he that is called of GOD, as was Aaron. (5) So also CHRIST glorified not HIMSELF to be made an high priest; but HE that said unto HIM, "THOU art MY SON, today have I begotten THEE". (6) As HE saith also in another place, "THOU art a priest forever after the order of Melchizedek", (7) WHO in the days of HIS flesh, when HE had offered up prayers and supplications with strong crying and tears unto HIM that was able to save HIM from death, and was heard in that HE feared; (8) Though HE were a SON, yet learned HE obedience by the things which HE suffered; (9) And being made perfect, HE became the author of eternal salvation unto all them that obey HIM; (10) Called of GOD an high priest after the order of Melchizek.

COMMENTARY:

In Hebrews chapters 4:14-5:10, the author seeks to show us how JESUS easily qualifies to fulfill the essentials of the priesthood, as they are defined by GOD. He thinks of the compassion of CHRIST as being far richer than the gentleness he ascribes to other high priests.

GOD declared and called CHRIST to be a Priest forever, in the order of Melchizedek. Earthly Priests were from the Levite line of Aaron, the line that was appointed by GOD to serve in the priesthood here on earth. Melchizedek, an obscure figure in Scriptures, was both a king and a Priest (Genesis 14:18-20), who ruled in Salem (now Jerusalem), during the time of Abraham.

Old Testament accounts make no mention of Melchizedek's father or mother. He seems to be without genealogy and, where his life begins, or ends, is unknown. However, there is one thing that is certain, and that is that, GOD knew him, and he knew GOD, and Abraham, knew them both. He was qualified to bless Abraham as a Priest, and to receive a tithe from Abraham as a king, who also, evidently, ranked higher spiritually, than did Abraham, and, Melchizedek remains a priest forever also (Hebrews 7:1-3).

In Psalms 110, a messianic psalm by David, Melchizedek is seen as a type of Christ. This theme is repeated here in this book of Hebrews, where both CHRIST and Melchizedek are considered as kings of righteousness and peace. In citing Melchizedek's unique priesthood as a prototype for CHRIST HIMSELF, the author is showing that CHRIST's priesthood is superior to the old Levitical order of Aaron also. And so, we see that a different kind of Priest has come, who became a Priest, not by meeting the old requirements of belonging to the tribe of Levi, but by the power of a life that cannot, and will not be destroyed, "a Priest forever, in the order of Melchizedek".

In Hebrews chapter 5, verse 2, as it is expressed in the original Greek, the word that the author of GOD uses for "compassion" is "metriopatheo" (met-ree-op-ath-eh-o), and it means "to be moderate in passion". It is the only time in scripture that this particular word is used for "compassion". We most often translate this word to mean, "to feel gently for". It is said that, somewhere in the midst of any two extremes, there can be found, "the right way". According to the Greeks, this is also where "virtue" can be discovered. They saw "virtue" as being the "midpoint" between two extremes.

Here in this passage the writer of Hebrews lists three important qualifications that any priest must satisfy;

• Compassion is one of those three essential qualifications. A Priest must be in full sympathy with others at all times, and ideally, should have gone through some of the same experiences as the people he seeks to council. If a person is not bound together with others in the trials that life brings, he will not be able to correctly sympathize with their plight, and therefore will not be able to grant sound advice.

• Secondly, Priests are appointed on behalf of others in order to deal with things concerning GOD. For instance, the earthly Priest was originally intended to be the link between the world and GOD. In the beginning, their primary function was to offer sacrifices to GOD for the sins of, first, himself, and then other people. The sacrifice was meant to restore a relationship with GOD that had been interrupted by sin.

- The third and most important qualification is that the Priest must be, "called by GOD", and not just show up, and appoint himself. The priesthood is a call to glory by GOD HIMSELF, and is not an office that is appointed by men.

GOD speaks to us, through our many experiences in life. These experiences always, in some way, try our hearts and souls. We can only hear HIS voice when we tune our minds to HIM, with complete "reverence". If we rebel against GOD, through our resentments, or "continuous sins", our hearts will build up a resistance that will make us deaf, or, unable to hear HIS voice.

JESUS, among HIS many roles, also serves as our "Eternal High Priest". HE has been exalted above the Heavens, and has no need to make sacrifices for us from day to day, like the old line of Levitical Priests had to do. Because of HIS vicarious sacrifice on the cross, HE, through GOD's grace, was able to cover the sins of every human being, past, present, and future, with HIS "Eternal Life-giving Blood".

A CALL TO SPIRITUAL GROWTH
Hebrews 5:11-6:12

5 (11) Of whom we have many things to say, and hard to be uttered, seeing ye are dull of hearing. (12) For when for the time ye ought to be teachers, ye have need that one teach you again which be the first principles of the oracles of GOD; and are become such as have need of milk, and not strong meat. (13) For everyone that useth milk is unskillful in the word of righteousness; for he is a babe. (14) But strong meat belongeth to them that are of full age, even those who by reason of use have their senses exercised to discern both good and evil.

Continue on reading in chapter six, verses 1-12

CHAPTER SIX:

A CALL FOR SPIRITUAL GROWTH (continued from chapter five)

SCRIPTURE:
The King James Version
Hebrews 6:1-12

6 (1) Therefore leaving the principles of the doctrine of CHRIST, let us go on unto perfection; not laying again the foundation of repentance from dead works, and of faith toward GOD, (2) Of the doctrine of baptisms, and of laying on of hands, and of resurrection of the dead, and of eternal judgment. (3) And this will we do, if GOD permit. (4) For it is impossible for those who were once enlightened, and have tasted of the heavenly gift, and were made partakers of the HOLY GHOST, (5) And have tasted the good word of GOD, and the powers of the world to come, (6) If we shall fall away, to renew them again unto repentance; seeing they crucify to themselves the SON of GOD afresh, and put HIM to an open shame. (7) For the earth which drinketh in the rain that cometh oft upon it, and bringeth forth herbs meet for them by WHOM it is dressed, receiveth blessing from GOD: (8) But that which beareth thorns and briers is rejected, and nigh unto cursing; whose end is to be burned, (9) But beloved, we are persuaded better things of you, and things that accompany salvation, though we thus speak. (10) For GOD is not unrighteous to forget your work and labour of love, which ye have shewed toward HIS name, in that ye have ministered to the saints, and do minister. (11) And we desire that every one of you do shew the same diligence to the full assurance of hope unto the end; (12) That ye be not slothful, but followers of them who through faith and patience inherit the promises.

COMMENTARY:

William E. Channing wrote, in his essay "Means of promoting Christianity", that, "The first laborers do little more than teach those who come after them, what to avoid, and how to labor more effectively than themselves". And it was A. Victor

Murry who wrote, "It doesn't matter how high a man's profession may be, it is by his actions that people judge him, and in judging him, they also judge his mentor. These two statements speak to the very essence of teaching, and learning what is taught. They can be applied to all facets of life.

In Hebrews 5:11- 6:12, the author of GOD challenges the readers with a call for spiritual growth. The Christian faith, in all its fullness, is by no means an easy thing to grasp. There is no way for it to be learned in short order, and, it is also true that, we as preachers and teachers often avoid learning and teaching some of the more difficult elements of the Bible.

In fact, one of the great tragedies of the African-American Christian church today, is that it seems to place more emphasis on race, and Sunday sermons, than it does on teaching the Word of GOD in Sunday school and weekly bible studies. A sermon does little, or nothing to edify the beliefs and hopes of a person who has no real knowledge of the things of GOD in them. It only serves to draw on peoples' emotions, or to entertain them for a very short space in time.

There is nothing more disenchanting than to walk into a well-established Christian congregation, and encounter the fact that most of the long term members are still on the "milk bottle of Christian knowledge and responsibility". We church leaders, who claim to be called by GOD, must begin to step up and shoulder the responsibility of feeding JESUS' sheep, especially those sheep who come to us voluntarily, without us ever having to take one step out of the church to round them up, and, who actually stay in our fold for years and years, and never experience Christian growth.

Do you love me? Is what JESUS asked Peter three times in John 21, and, I guess the only way to prove our love for JESUS is by loving others, and also by "feeding HIS sheep" with the nourishing food of the word of GOD. In Matthew 28:19-20, JESUS commands us to "Go ye therefore, and teach all nations, baptizing them in the name of the FATHER, and of the SON, and of the HOLY GHOST: Teaching them to observe all things whatsoever I have commanded you: and, lo, I am with you always, even unto the end of the world" (KJV).

In the Greek, the word used for "perfect" is "teleios" (tel-i-os), and it is "to be of full age or maturity". It is "to be mature in the various applications of life, including physical, mental, moral and spiritual growth", and it also means, in the spiritual sense, "to fully realize the purpose for which you came into the world". For every man, woman, and child, that purpose is to come to know, accept, and serve GOD in all HIS fullness, and to love one another enough to want to teach each and every person you meet, about CHRIST and the Word of GOD. And so we see, in the biblical sense, "perfection" is a "functional achievement", not an abstract, or metaphysical pursuit, or aspiration. This is clearly what JESUS means when HE encourages us to be "perfect" (Matthew 5:48 & 19:21, Luke 7:40, John 17:23, & 2 Corinthians 12:9).

In Hebrews 5:11, as expressed in the original Greek writing, the word the author uses for "dull of hearing" is "nothros" (no-thros), and it means slow-moving in mind, sluggish in understanding, or stupidly forgetful. Here the writer clearly seeks to arouse the consciousness of his readers. He wants to stir them out of their spiritual naps, or doldrums, where they were quite literally sleeping on the ABC's of the Holy Scriptures.

When we as Christians, who have tasted the free gift that comes from heaven, shared in the HOLY SPIRIT, tasted the fair Word of GOD, and, tasted the powers of the world to come, fall back into sin because of our laziness and refusal to grow spiritually, we, in effect, are crucifying JESUS all over again.

There can be no "inertia" in the Christian walk, nor can the Christian ever afford to take a balcony view to life and sit and watch the world go by. We must take advantage of every opportunity we get to learn more about the Word of GOD, so that we will be able to share that Word, more effectively with others whom we encounter from day to day, just as JESUS commands us to do. The fact that we cast everything, over to GOD, does not give us a right to sit back and do nothing.

GOD'S PROMISES BRING HOPE
Hebrews 6:13-20

6 (13) For when GOD made promise to Abraham, because HE could swear by no greater, HE sware by HIMSELF. (14) Saying, "Surely blessing I will bless thee, and multiplying I will multiply thee". (15) And so, after he had patiently endured, he obtained the promise. (16) For men verily swear by the greater: and an oath for confirmation is to them an end to all strife. (17) Wherein GOD, willing more abundantly to shew unto the heirs of promise the immutability of his counsel, confirmed it by oath: (18) That by two immutable things, in which it was impossible for GOD to lie, we might have a strong consolation, who have fled for refuge to lay hold upon the hope set before us: (19) Which hope we have as an anchor of the soul, both sure and stedfast, and which entereth into that within the veil: (20) Whither the forerunner is for us entered, even JESUS, made an high priest for ever after the order of Melchizedek.

COMMENTARY:

In the New Testament Greek, the word used here in this passage for "oath" is "horkos", and it is indicative of a solemn, legally binding pledge that guarantees that a person will keep their promise. There are many biblical passages that tell of GOD swearing an oath (Luke 1:73, Acts 2:30, Hebrews 3:11, 4:3, 7:20-22), and GOD's reason for doing this, is to stress HIS intentions, and, to give us a strong basis to believe that all HE has promised us will come to pass in the process of time. GOD made a promise to save all of those, who believe in HIS SON, CHRIST JESUS, and, we need not fear or doubt any of HIS promises regarding this revelation, or, in fact, anything else HE has promised us, because GOD, quite simply, cannot lie.

If a person needs to find a model who can personify the patience, confidence, and trust in a promise of GOD, one only needs to look at the example of Abraham. Abraham patiently awaited GOD's promise of a great nation through his seed, and in the process of time, his patience was rewarded. And even though Abraham did not get to see the fullness and completion of the promise, he did get to see its beginnings and he trusted in his heart that GOD would complete HIS promise to him, through his son Isaac and his heirs.

GOD's promise to Abraham was not just for the benefit of Abraham, but it was also for the benefit of all Christians in general, through CHRIST JESUS, WHO would come through his line to save us all. GOD's Word, and GOD's oath are the two great unchangeable things, and they are also the motivation behind the Christian Hope. In fact, they allow us to take hold of that Christian Hope and cling to it as a fortified refuse in times of trouble.

JESUS' entry into the Heavenly sanctuary to serve as our HIGH PRIEST, gives Christians an anchor of hope that can never be shaken loose from the Kingdom of GOD. JESUS, as our "forerunner" is the imagery of a sailor who has been designated to leave the ship, and go out in a small boat, in order to drop the ship's anchor in a firm lodging place. That is what JESUS did for us, through HIS vicarious sacrifice at Golgotha, so that we could have firm safe refuse in Heaven at the end of our journey.

WHAT DID WE LEARN FROM CHAPTERS 4-6?
Here are some key points to remember

(1). Peace is achieved through one's belief in, and obedience to, GOD.

(Hebrews 4:1-11)

(2). Nothing in creation can hide from GOD, and we must all make an account for the deeds done in our lifetimes. (Hebrews 4:12)

(3). JESUS understands our weaknesses because HE faced all of the same temptations we that we do, and, HE overcame them. (Hebrews 4:15-5:2)

(4). JESUS is our HIGH PRIEST, chosen by GOD, and HE offered up HIMSELF as a sacrifice for our sins. (Hebrews 5:5-10)

(5). We must not become stagnant in our Christian walk, but rather, we must continue to grow and mature in our knowledge and service of GOD. (Hebrews 5:11-6:3)

(6). There is no "unconditional security" apart from "true salvation". In other words, a person is mocking GOD when they pledge themselves to HIM, and then, go out and continue the kind of lifestyle that they lived before their pledge. Such people are condemning themselves to Hell, by nailing CHRIST to the cross all over again. (Hebrews 6:4-7)

(7). GOD has given us both HIS promise and HIS oath, to deliver us into HIS place of rest if we choose CHRIST JESUS, WHO can save us. And because GOD cannot lie, we can all come to rest in the thought that this promise will remain unchangeable unto eternal life. (Hebrews 6:13-20)

CHAPTER SEVEN:

JESUS: A GREATER PRIEST WITH A GREATER MINISTRY

SCRIPTURE:
The King James Version
Hebrews 7

7 (1) For this Melchizedek, king of Salem, priest of the MOST HIGH GOD, who met Abraham returning from the slaughter of the kings, and blessed him; (2) To whom Abraham gave a tenth part of all; first being by interpretation king of righteousness, and after that also king of Salem, which is, king of peace; (3) Without father, without mother, without descent, having neither beginning of days, nor end of life; but made like unto the SON of GOD; abideth a priest continually. (4) Now consider how great this man was, unto whom even the patriarch Abraham gave the tenth of the spoils. (5) And verily they that are of the sons of Levi, who receive the office of the priesthood, have a commandment to take tithes of the people according to the law, that is, of their brethren, though they come out of the loins of Abraham: (6) But he whose descent is not counted from them received tithes of Abraham, and blessed him that had the promises. (7) And without all contradiction the less is blessed of the better. (8) And here men that die receive tithes; but there he receiveth them, of whom it is witnessed that he liveth. (9) And as I may so say, Levi also, who receiveth tithes, payed tithes in Abraham. (10) For he was yet in the loins of his father, when Melchizedek met him. (11) If therefore perfection where by the Levitical priesthood, (for under it the people received the law,) what further need was there that another priest should rise after the order of Melchizedek, and not be called after the order of Aaron? (12) For the priesthood being changed, there is made of necessity a change also of the law. (13) For he of whom these things are spoken pertaineth to another tribe, of which no man gave attendance at the altar. (14) For it is evident that our LORD sprang out of Juda; of which tribe Moses spake nothing concerning priesthood. (15) And it is yet far evident; for that after the similitude of Melchizedek there ariseth another PRIEST. (16) WHO is made, not after the law of a carnal commandment, but after the power of an endless life. (17) For he testifieth, "THOU art a priest forever after the order of Melchizedek. (18) For there is verily a disannulling of the commandment going before for the weakness and unprofitableness thereof. (19) For the law made nothing perfect, but the bringing in of a better hope did; by which we draw near unto GOD.

(20) And inasmuch as not without an oath he was made priest: (21) (For those priest were made without an oath; but this with an oath by HIM that said unto HIM, "the LORD sware and will not repent, THOU art a priest forever after the order of Melchizedek:) (22) By so much was JESUS made a surety of a better testament. (23) And they truly were many priests, because they were not suffered to continue by reason of death: (24) But this MAN, because HE continueth ever, hath an unchangeable priesthood. (25) Wherefore HE is able also to save them to the uttermost that come unto GOD by HIM, seeing HE ever liveth to make intercession for them. (26) For such an HIGH PRIEST became us, WHO is holy, harmless, undefiled, separate from sinners, and made higher than the heavens; (27) WHO needeth not daily, as those high priests, to offer up sacrifice, first for his own sins, and then for the people's; for this HE did once, when HE offered up HIMSELF. (28) For the law maketh men high priests which have infirmity; but the word of oath, which was since the law, maketh the SON, WHO is consecrated for evermore.

COMMENTARY:

Way back in Genesis 14, after Abraham (then Abram) had defeated a band of armies led by King Kedorlaomer of Elam, and rescued his nephew Lot from certain doom, we are introduced to one of the most obscure, and yet, important figures in the annals of Old Testament history.

Upon Abraham's return from battle, he is met by a man named Melchizedek in the valley of Shaveh. Melchizedek was the King of Salem (now Jerusalem) and was also a priest of our GOD Most High. His name means "king of justice", and the name of his kingdom, "Salem", means "peace". And so, by his very name and position he was both, "king of justice", and, "king of peace". He was also high enough in stature and importance, that, he could both, bless Abraham, and, receive a tithe from Abraham.

Here in Hebrews chapter 7, the author emphasizes the fact that JESUS' priesthood does not derive from Aaron's Levitical line of priests, but rather, it derives from the line of Melchizedek, a superior priesthood. In verses 1-10, the author establishes two things.

- First, the greater always blesses the lesser. Here the author is showing that, by blessing Abraham, Melchizedek was greater than Abraham.
- And secondly, Abraham, who was the great, great-grandfather of Aaron, the first of the Levitical line of priests, paid a tithe to Melchizedek, and thus personally acknowledged the superiority of his priesthood.

As, it is written by king David in his prophetic Psalm 110:4, GOD's ordaining someone as a "priest forever in the line of Melchizedek" is a clear indication that GOD always intended to make a change in the Aaronic priesthood. And such a change would also require a change in the whole system of the Mosiac Law, of which that priesthood was a part (Vs. 11-19).

JESUS' priesthood is better simply because it is flawless, and it is forever, or, eternal. In the Old Testament, you'll find that, neither Melchizedek's birth, nor his death, are recorded. There is no record of his father or mother or any of his ancestors, and no beginning or end to his life. He remains a priest forever resembling the SON of GOD. His priesthood is also permanent, just as JESUS lives eternally as our Heavenly priest, and, can save us continuously and completely.

JESUS' priesthood is able to meet our needs, by way of HIS vicarious sacrifice, which settles forever, the issue of our sins. HE is the only one WHO can speak for us, and intercede for us before GOD the FATHER. The priesthood of CHRIST differs dramatically from the Levitical priesthood, in that, it was instituted with an oath. By contrast, the descendants of Aaron assumed their jobs without any oath.

In the Greek, the word used in Hebrews 7:22 for "surety" is "engyos". This is the only time this particular word is used in New Testament scriptures. It is a legal term which identifies a bond or collateral. It means that the signer of the guarantee pledged his resources as security for the commitment that is made. JESUS is the living guarantee that the forgiveness GOD offers us under the New Covenant will surely be ours. In fact, because of HIS oath, HE became the guarantee of a better Covenant. With HIS OWN life, JESUS assured the superiority of the new order over the old, because HIS oath also secured HIS permanent installation in the priestly office of GOD.

No Old Testament priest ever functioned in this permanent manner, simply because, all of them were subject to death and mortality. JESUS not only prays for us,

HE also has empowered us to live a more righteous life here on earth, through HIS examples and gift of the HOLY SPIRIT. As an ever-living HIGH PRIEST, JESUS is always available to represent us before GOD, and thus, HE is able to save us completely.

Remember, everyone who has been saved by CHRIST, was saved when they were still sinners. When we stumble after receiving salvation, JESUS remains there with us to keep us from falling, because HE is always holding us by the hand. HE remains committed to us so that HE can save us completely. If salvation depended on us, then, we would have a right to worry. But, because salvation depends on JESUS, we can be free from fret and worry, because our futures are completely secure, through HIM.

WHAT DID WE LEARN FROM CHAPTER SEVEN?
Here are some key points to remember

(1). Melchizedek was a priest who was modeled after JESUS. (Hebrews 7:1-3)
(2). Abraham paid tithes to GOD through Melchizedek. (Hebrews 7:2)
(3). Melchizedek was great enough to bless Abraham, who was the holder of GOD's promise. (Hebrews 7:6b)
(4). JESUS CHRIST is an eternal priest in the line of Melchizedek. (Hebrews 7:11)
(5). JESUS represents a change and improvement from the Levite priesthood of Aaron. (Hebrews 7:12-14)
(6). JESUS does not need to continuously offer sacrifices to GOD for our sins like earthly priests do, because HE HIMSELF, is the perfect sacrifice WHO has already been offered up on the cross, once, and for all time. (Hebrews 7:27)

CHAPTER EIGHT:

THE SUPERIOR SERVICE OF CHRIST

SCRIPTURE:
The King James Version
Hebrews 8

8 (1) Now of the things which we have spoken this is the sum: We have such an HIGH PRIEST, WHO is set on the right hand of the throne of the MAJESTY in the heavens; (2) A MINISTER of the Sanctuary, and true Tabernacle, which the LORD pitched, and not man. (3) For every high priest is ordained to offer gifts and sacrifices: wherefore it is of necessity that this man have somewhat also to offer. (4) For if HE were on earth, HE should not be a priest, seeing that there are priests that offer gifts according to the law: (5) Who serve unto the example and shadow of Heavenly things, as Moses was admonished of GOD when he was about to make the tabernacle: for, see, saith HE, "That thou make all things according to the pattern shewed to thee in the mount", (6) But now hath HE obtained a more excellent ministry, by how much also HE is the mediator of a better covenant, which was established upon better promises. (7) For if that first covenant had been faultless, then should no place have been sought for the second. (8) For finding fault with them, HE saith, "Behold, the days come, saith the LORD, when I will make a new covenant with the house of Israel and with the house of Judah: (9) Not according to the covenant that I made with their fathers in the day when I took them by the hand to lead them out of the land of Egypt; because they continued not in MY covenant, and I regarded them not, saith the LORD. (10) For this is the covenant that I will make with the house of Israel after those days, saith the LORD; I will put MY laws into their hearts: and I will be to them a GOD, and they shall be to ME a people: (11) And they shall not teach every man his neighbor, and every man his brother, saying, know the LORD: for all shall know ME, from the least to the greatest. (12) For I will be merciful to their unrighteousness, and their sins and their iniquities will I remember no more". (13) In that HE saith, "A new covenant", He hath made the first old. Now that which decayeth and waxeth old is ready to vanish away.

COMMENTARY:

JESUS ministers on the basis of a better covenant. HE is GOD's superior priest and our ultimate representative in the presence of the FATHER in Heaven. A superior priest could never operate on the basis of an inferior covenant. Here in chapter 8, the writer begins to move toward the conclusion of his discussion and argument regarding the superiority of CHRIST JESUS as our HIGH PRIEST.

Aaronic priests ministered on earth in a sanctuary that was a mere copy of the Heavenly Sanctuary. It was only a shadow of the true sanctuary in Heaven that was built by the hand of GOD, and where CHRIST now ministers. The superiority of JESUS' ministry is also reflected in the superiority of the New Covenant, which HE ushered in to us, during HIS three-year ministry here on earth.

Unlike the earthly high priest who was required to offer gifts and sacrifices for, first, their own sins, and then ours, JESUS has no need to offer sacrifices for HIMSELF because HE, quite frankly has never sinned. And the sacrifice HE offers for our sins, past, present, and future, is HIS OWN life, which was offered up on the cross at Golgotha, where HE spilled HIS blood, some 2000 years ago.

Back in Exodus 24, verses 1-8, the Israelites accepted GOD's covenant as it had been given to Moses on Mount Sinai. However, man would not then, and quite frankly, will not now, abide by such a covenant, because we let our sins continuously interrupt our relationship with GOD.

It took the life of CHRIST to restore our lost relationship of friendship with GOD. If we, as a people, would have abided by the first covenant, there would have been no need for the, more superior covenant that was ushered in by CHRIST JESUS to replace it.

The first covenant was offered by GOD to show us how much we need HIM in our lives to survive, and, how far we were from living according to HIS OWN glorious standards. Therefore, as a result, the old Covenant, in essence, could only condemn us. The New Covenant, by contrast, brings forgiveness through CHRIST JESUS, and thereby, can only save us. However, this salvation can only be given to those who voluntarily accept GOD, in all HIS fullness.

In the Greek, the word used for "covenant", in all normal secular applications, is "suntheke" (soon-tha-kay), and it is "an agreement between two equal parties or entities, on equal terms", i.e. a marriage, or a business deal or partnership.

However, in the New Testament Scriptures, the Greek word that is always used for "covenant" is "diatheke" (dee-ath-ay-kay), and it is "an agreement that is actually along the terms of a "devised Will". In other words, only one party draws up the terms (GOD), and the other party (mankind) can either accept or reject the terms, or inheritance, that is offered. They cannot change or alter any of the contents within that Will. The choice of this word, (diatheke), is understandable, because we, as human beings, cannot enter into an equal partnership with GOD, and cannot be on equal terms with GOD for obvious reasons. We are only able to make a voluntary decision to accept, or reject HIS covenant offer, and cannot alter, or change HIS terms in any way.

Even in the secular world, we know that a Will does not go into effect until the person who wrote it has been proven dead. JESUS, WHO is our HIGH PRIEST, first died on the cross for our sins, then, re-entered into Heaven itself, bearing HIS OWN blood to present as a sacrificial atonement for all of our sins, past, present, and future. And with HIS sacrifice, HE purchased eternal salvation for all mankind in general, and all Christians in particular, once, and for all time. In short, JESUS is the mediator of the New Covenant that was activated by HIS OWN death.

In the Greek, there are two words that are used for "new". One is "neos" (neh-os), which is "new in respects to time". It can be a regeneration, or "exact copy" of something already existing, such as a new piece of clothing, or a new pair of shoes.

The other word used for "new" is "kainos" (kahee-nos), which means, not only new in relation to time, but also new in quality and expression. It is something that is a new creation altogether, or a new product that has been introduced into the world for the first time. "Kainos" is the word used here by the author to describe the covenant ushered in by JESUS CHRIST. However, this New Covenant ushered in by CHRIST can never be improved upon, or copied.

There is one other essential that we should accentuate regarding the New Covenant. In Hebrews 10:16-18, the author of GOD tells us that the New Covenant is one that calls for "internal", rather than "external" adaptations. This means that people would no longer want to obey GOD simply because the law compels them to, or they fear punishment, but rather, because the desire to obey HIM will be written on their hearts and minds.

Under the old Covenant, man could only hope to keep a right relationship with GOD by obeying HIS laws, through their own efforts. Here, in the New Covenant Age, everything is dependent, not on, what we can do, but rather, everything rests solely on the grace of GOD, and what JESUS CHRIST has done, by way of HIS vicarious sacrifice. JESUS, both, removes our guilt, and, mediates our New Covenant with GOD.

With the coming of the New Covenant, GOD wishes to place HIS laws for living on our hearts, not just in writing on stone or, even paper, for that matter. HE wants us to understand HIM in our innermost being, so that we can obey HIM more completely. HE wants to be our GOD, and HE wants us to be HIS people. HE wants us to teach of HIM, not just with the words of our mouths, but more importantly, with our behavior as professed Christians.

We, as Christians, must make our old selves obsolete, just as GOD made the Old Covenant Law obsolete when HE sent us HIS only begotten SON to save us from ourselves. In the New Testament Greek, the word used for "old", or "obsolete" is "palaioumenon" (pal-ah-yo-o-me-non), and it describes "something that is out of date" and "ready to be set aside".

WHAT DID WE LEARN FROM CHAPTER EIGHT?
Here are some key points to remember

(1). JESUS is our high priest, and now ministers in the sacred tent in Heaven, the true place of worship, that was built by the hands of GOD, and not by human hands. (Hebrews 8:1-2)

(2). Earthly priests serve in a place of worship that is only a copy of the real place of worship that is in Heaven. (Hebrews 8:5a)

(3). GOD gave Moses instructions on how to build a replica of the place of worship in Heaven. (Hebrews 8:5b)

(4). JESUS was given, by GOD, a superior ministry to the ones of the earthly priests, who, serve under the old law. (Hebrews 8:6)

(5). Through CHRIST, and the HOLY SPIRIT, GOD puts HIS laws in our minds and, writes them on our hearts, so that we may understand, and, choose to obey HIM instinctively. (Hebrews 8:8-12)

(6). The Old Covenant Law, which was ushered in through Moses, has been replaced, by the New Covenant of Grace, that was ushered in by CHRIST JESUS. (Hebrews 8:13)

CHAPTER NINE:

(30)

OLD RULES ABOUT WORSHIP

SCRIPTURE:
The King James Version
Hebrews 9:1-10

9 (1) Then verily the first covenant had also ordinances of divine service, and a worldly sanctuary. (2) For there was a tabernacle made; the first, wherein was the candlestick, and the table, and the showbread; which is called the sanctuary. (3) And after the second veil, the tabernacle which is called the Holiest of all; (4) Which had the golden censer, and the ark of the covenant overlaid round about with gold, wherein was the golden pot that had manna, and Aaron's rod that budded, and the tables of the covenant; (5) And over it the cherubims of glory shadowing the mercy seat; of which we cannot now speak particularly. (6) Now when these things were thus ordained, the priests went always into the first tabernacle, accomplishing the service of GOD. (7) But into the second went the high priest alone once every year, not without blood, which he offered for himself, and for the errors of the people: (8) The HOLY GHOST this signifying, that the way into the holiest of all was not yet made manifest, while as the first tabernacle was yet standing: (9) Which was a figure for the time then present, in which were offered both gifts and sacrifices, that could not make him that did the service perfect, as pertaining to the conscience; (10) Which stood only in meats and drinks, and divers washings, and carnal ordinances, imposed on them until the time of reformation.

COMMENTARY:

In Hebrews chapter 9, the writer expands on his argument concerning the superiority of the New Covenant that was ushered in by CHRIST JESUS. In the first covenant between GOD and Israel (the Mosaic Covenant), there were many regulations concerning worship, and, there was a sacred place, a tent, in which to do it. Every element of the Mosaic Covenant had special significance because it reflected realities that are found only in Heaven. Inside this sacred tent were two rooms. In the first room there was a lamp stand, a table, and loaves of holy bread on the table, and it was called, the "Holy Place".

Now there was a curtain that separated this first room from a second room. This second room was called the "Most Holy Place". Inside this second room, were a gold incense altar and a wooden chest called the "Ark of the Covenant". The Ark was covered with gold on all sides, and inside it were three items, a gold jar, which contained the two quarts of manna that were placed there by Aaron at the command of GOD, through Moses (Exodus 16:32-34). There was also Aaron's blooming staff, which GOD commanded to be put there as a warning to those who try to rebel against HIM (Numbers 17:10-11). And, there were the tablets upon which the Ten Commandments were written (Exodus 40:20).

Above the ark were angels whose wings were stretched out over the Ark's cover, the place of atonement. Any of the priests were able to go in and out of the first room on a regular basis, as they performed their religious duties to man and GOD. However, only the high priest was allowed to enter into the second room, the Most Holy Place, and then, he could enter it only once a year, always with blood that would be offered up to GOD to cover, first, his own sins, and then, the sins of the people.

By these regulations, the HOLY SPIRIT was communicating that the Most Holy Place was not open to everyone, as long as the first room, the Holy Place, and all that it represents, was still in use. This was also an illustration of how the gifts and sacrifices that the priests were offering were not able to cleanse the consciences of the people that brought them.

This old system only dealt with food, drink, ritual washing, and other external regulations that were, in effect, only until their limitations could be corrected by the introduction of the New Covenant, that was ushered in by JESUS CHRIST. All of the old system's Levitical arrangements were designed to convey the idea that the true way to GOD did not lie in them, but rather, would lie in CHRIST. What this tells us in this day and age, is that, the old covenant sacrificial system never met our human needs on their most profound level, and could not, by any means, clear the spiritual consciences of the people who seek to worship GOD.

JESUS IS THE PERFECT SACRIFICE
Hebrews 9:11-28

9 (11) But CHRIST being come an high priest of good things to come, by a greater and more perfect tabernacle, not made with hands, that is to say, not of this building; (12) Neither by the blood of goats and calves, but by HIS OWN blood HE entered in once into the Holy Place, having obtained eternal redemption for us. (13) For if the blood of bulls and of goats, and the ashes of an heifer sprinkling the unclean, sanctifieth to the purifying of the flesh: (14) How much more shall the blood of CHRIST, WHO through the ETERNAL SPIRIT offered HIMSELF without spot to GOD, purge your conscience from dead works to serve the living GOD? (15) And for this cause HE is the mediator of the New Testament, that by means of death, for the redemption of the transgressions that were under the first Testament, they which are called might receive the promise of eternal inheritance. (16) For where a Testament is, there must also of necessity be the death of a Testator. (17) For a Testament is of force after men are dead: otherwise it is of no strength at all while the Testator liveth. (18) Whereupon neither the first Testament was dedicated without blood. (19) For when Moses had spoken every precept to all the people according to the law, he took the blood of calves and of goats, with water, and scarlet wool, and hyssop, and sprinkled both the book, and all the people, (20) Saying, "This is the blood of the Testament which GOD hath enjoined unto you". (21) Moreover he sprinkled with blood both the tabernacle, and all the vessels of the ministry. (22) And almost all things are by the law purged with blood; and without shedding of blood is no remission. (23) It is therefore necessary that the patterns of things in the heavens should be purified with these; but the heavenly things themselves with better sacrifices than these. (24) For CHRIST is not entered into the holy places made with hands, which are the figures of the true; but into Heaven itself, now to appear in the presence of GOD for us: (25) Nor yet that HE should offer HIMSELF often, as the high priest entereth into the holy place every year with blood of others; (26) For then must HE often have suffered since the foundation of the world: but now once in the end of the world hath HE appeared to put away sin by the sacrifice of HIMSELF. (27) And as it is appointed unto men once to die, but after this the judgment: (28) So CHRIST was once offered to bear the sins of many; and unto them that look for HIM shall HE appear the second time without sin unto salvation.

COMMENTARY:

JESUS CHRIST has now entered into the perfect sanctuary that was not made by human hands, but rather, by the hand of GOD. There HE has become high priest over all that is good. Once and for all time HE has carried HIS OWN blood into the Most Holy Place in Heaven, and with it, HE has secured our salvation forever.

Under the old law, the blood of goats, bulls, or rams could be used to cleanse the defilement of human sins. How much more effective then, must the blood of CHRIST be in purifying the human heart from deeds that had long led man to death, and is now allowing man to re-establish a relationship of friendship with GOD.

Here in chapter 9, the writer prompts his readers to recall that all elements of the Mosaic Covenant had special meaning in that, it reflected the realities in Heaven. But our HIGH PRIEST, JESUS, entered into Heaven itself, bearing HIS OWN blood, and by HIS OWN sacrifice, obtained for us, the greatest gift of all time, salvation. JESUS is the mediator of the New Covenant, a covenant that was activated by HIS OWN death on the cross.

In Old Testament times, animal blood sacrifices were the standard requirement by GOD for the sins of man. In essence, it indicates that sin merits death, but GOD is willing to accept a substitute in place of the life of the sinner. Hebrews chapters 8-10 teaches us that the system of Old Testament sacrifices was actually an "object lesson" used by GOD to aid us in the understanding of the coming sacrifice of HIS only begotten SON, JESUS, the CHRIST.

The Old Testament sacrifices had an external effectiveness, but JESUS' sacrifice at Golgotha has an internal effect that cleanses the conscience that bounds us to the guilt of our past. We are no longer overcome with a past that renders us inadequate to function in the present, and keeps us from moving forward to a brighter future with GOD.

When a person dies and leaves a will, no one can collect on the benefits of that will until there is proof that the person who wrote that will is actually dead. Likewise, under the old covenant, GOD required the blood of certain animals as proof of death, and the blood confirmed man's obedience to the covenant. Afterwards, man was able to collect on the benefits of GOD's will, which was found in HIS forgiveness, instead of the death of the sinner.

The blood of animals was sufficient to purify things here on earth, and by the sprinkling of animal blood, man was allowed to continue to live here on earth. However, the real things, which are only found in Heaven, had to be purified with a far better sacrifice than the blood of unblemished animals. It took the blood of an unblemished man to meet the requirement of GOD to enter into the Kingdom of Heaven, and that perfect sacrifice could only come in the person of JESUS CHRIST.

But first, JESUS had to become a man (100% human), born into the world like all other men, so that HE could suffer through everything man has to suffer through, overcome it, and then, present HIMSELF faultless before HIS FATHER GOD as the perfect sacrifice for the sin atonement of all persons, past, present, and future, once and for all time.

And just as it is appointed by GOD that each person dies only once, and after which comes judgment, so too, CHRIST died only once as a sacrifice that took away the sins of the people who choose to believe in HIM. JESUS will come again, but not to deal with our sins again. This time HE will bring with HIM, the salvation that is promised to all those who believe, and eagerly await HIS return.

WHAT DID WE LEARN FROM CHAPTER NINE?
Here are some key points to remember

(1). In the first covenant between GOD and Israel there were regulations for worship and a sacred tent with two rooms in it, that were separated by a curtain. (Hebrews 9:1-3)

(2). The first room was called the Holy Place, and the second room was called the Most Holy Place. (Hebrews 9:2-3)

(3). The "Ark of the Covenant" was kept in the Most Holy Place. (Hebrews 9:4)

(4). Inside the Ark there were three items; a gold jar containing manna, Aaron's budding staff, and the stone tablets upon which the Ten Commandments were written. (Hebrews 9:4)

(5). Any priest could go in and out of the first room, the Holy Place, on a regular basis, as they performed their religious duties. (Hebrews 9:6)

(6). Only the high priest could enter into the Most Holy Place, and then, only once a year with blood offerings for the sins of himself, and, the people. (Hebrews 9:7)

(7). The gifts and sacrifices of the people were not enough to cleanse their consciences, because the old covenant only dealt with the external things. (Hebrews 9:9)

(8). The New Covenant, ushered in by CHRIST, WHO was the perfect sacrifice, cleanses the hearts of men from the deeds that lead to death, thereby making it possible for us to worship the LIVING GOD. (Hebrews 9:11-15)

(9). Blood was required by GOD, under the old covenant, as proof of death and it confirmed HIS covenant with Israel. (Hebrews 9:18)

(10). Without the shedding of blood there could be no forgiveness of sin, because the price of sin is death. (Hebrews 9:22)

(11). JESUS' sacrificial death on the cross, and the shedding of HIS blood, atoned for the sins of man, past, present, and future, once, and for all times. (Hebrews 9:24-28)

(12). JESUS was the perfect sacrifice. (Hebrews 9:11-28)

CHAPTER TEN:

ONCE AND FOR ALL

SCRIPTURE
The King James Version
Hebrews 10:1-18

10 (1) For the law having a shadow of good things to come, and not the very image of the things, can never with those sacrifices which they offered year by year continually make the comers thereunto perfect. (2) For then would they not have ceased to be offered? Because that the worshippers once purged should have had no more conscience of sins. (3) But in those sacrifices there is a remembrance again made of sins every year. (4) For it is not possible that the blood of bulls and of goats should take away sins. (5) Wherefore when HE cometh into the world, HE saith, "Sacrifice and offering thou wouldest not, but a body hast thou prepared ME: (6) In burnt offerings and sacrifices for sin thou hast had no pleasure. (7) Then said I, lo, I come (in the volume of the book it is written of ME,) to do THY will, o GOD." (8) Above when HE said, "Sacrifice and offering and burnt offerings and offering for sin thou wouldest not, neither hadst pleasure therein;" which are offered by the law; (9) Then said HE, "Lo, I come to do THY will, O GOD, HE taketh away the first, that HE may establish the second. (10) By the which will we are sanctified through the offering of the body of JESUS CHRIST once for all. (11) And every priest standeth daily ministering and offering oftentimes the same sacrifices, which can never take away sins: (12) But this MAN, after HE had offered one sacrifice for sins for ever sat down on the right hand of GOD; (13) From henceforth expecting till HIS enemies are made HIS footstool. (14) For by one offering HE hath perfected for ever them that are sanctified. (15) Whereof the HOLY GHOST also is a witness to us: for after that HE had said before, (16) "This is the covenant that I will make with them after those days, saith the LORD, I will put MY laws into their hearts, and in their minds will I write them; (17) And their sins and iniquities will I remember no more". (18) Now where remission of these is, there is no more offering for sin.

COMMENTARY:

The old sacrificial system contained in the Mosaic Law was only a shadow of the things to come. Through it, we could not really grasp the realities of the good things that CHRIST JESUS has done for us. The sacrifices under the old system had to be repeated over and over again, year after year, and still, were not able to provide perfect cleansing for those who came to worship. If the old system sacrifices could have provided perfect cleansing, they would not have had to be repeated over and over again, because the worshipers would have been purified once and for all time.

Hebrews chapter 10 is the final subsection of the writer's expository unit regarding the superiority of CHRIST, which he began in chapter seven. Here he argues that the superior sacrifice of CHRIST is what now perfects the New-Covenant worshipper. We are, by JESUS' vicarious sacrifice, purified once and for all time.

The old system of sacrifice really served as more of an annual reminder of sin, than anything else it represented. GOD wishes for us to worship HIM with the minds, hearts, and bodies, which HE has given us, and not with the blood of dead animals, nor with grain offerings. GOD wants us to worship HIM in "spirit and in truth", not in "ritual".

Like CHRIST JESUS, we must all come to do GOD's will with our whole bodies. JESUS CHRIST, through HIS vicarious sacrifice, has canceled the Old Covenant and put into effect, HIS New Covenant. "Eis to dienekes" is the Greek phrase that the writer of Hebrews uses repeatedly regarding JESUS' continuing sacrificial effect on human destiny during the course of his argument in chapters 7-10. This phrase means "forever", or, "continuously and uninterruptedly". JESUS CHRIST continuously and uninterruptedly guarantees the New Covenant promise.

JESUS came to usher in a New Covenant from GOD. It is a Covenant that is far superior to any before, or since that time. It is now the duty of the Christian to build his or her foundation on the "Most-High Faith" of the MOST HIGH PRIEST. We have to learn to pray in the power of the HOLY SPIRIT, and to remember the conditions of that New Covenant, under which the love of GOD has called us. And after we have done all that we can, we are still at the mercy of JESUS CHRIST unto eternal life.

No one goes the FATHER, but by JESUS. HE alone, is THE WAY to GOD. In HIM, we see exactly what GOD is like, and only HE can usher us into GOD's OWN glorious presence, without fear, without guilt, and, without shame.

A CALL TO PERSEVERE
Hebrews 10:19-39

10 (19) Having therefore, brethren, boldness to enter into the holiest by the blood of JESUS, (20) By a new and living way, which HE hath consecrated for us, through the veil, that is to say, HIS flesh; (21) And having an high priest over the house of GOD; (22) Let us draw near with a true heart in full assurance of faith, having our hearts sprinkled from an evil conscience, and our bodies washed with pure water. (23) Let us hold fast the profession of our faith without wavering; (for HE is faithful that promised;) (24) And let us consider one another to provoke unto love and to good works: (25) Not forsaking the assembling of ourselves together, as the manner of some is; but exhorting one another: and so much the more, as ye see the day approaching. (26) For if we sin willfully after that we have received the knowledge of the truth, there remaineth no more sacrifice for sins, (27) But a certain fearful looking for of judgment and fiery indignation, which shall devour the adversaries. (28) He that despised Moses' law died without mercy under two or three witnesses: (29) Of how much sorer punishment, suppose ye, shall he be thought worthy, who hath trodden under foot the SON of GOD, and hath counted the blood of the covenant, wherewith he was sanctified, an unholy thing, and hath done despite unto the SPIRIT of grace? (30) For we know HIM that hath said, "Vengeance belongeth unto ME, I will recompense, saith the LORD". And again, "The LORD shall judge HIS people". (31) It is a fearful thing to fall into the hands of the LIVING GOD. (32) But call to remembrance the former days, in which, after ye were illuminated, ye endured a great fight of afflictions; (33) Partly, whilst ye were made a gazingstock both by reproaches and afflictions; and partly, whilst ye became companions of them that were so used. (34) For ye had compassion of me in my bonds, and took joyfully the spoiling of your goods, knowing in yourselves that ye have in Heaven a better and an enduring substance. (35) Cast not away therefore your confidence, which hath great recompense of reward. (36) For ye have need of patience, that, after ye have done the will of GOD, ye might receive the promise. (37) For yet a little while, and HE that shall come will come, and will not tarry. (38) Now the just shall live by faith: but if any man draw back, MY soul shall have no pleasure in

him. (39) But we are not of them who draw back unto perdition; but of them
that believe to the saving of the soul.

COMMENTARY:

The Old Covenant imagery of the curtain, in the Holy Place, that, once served as a barrier to man has been erased by the sacrificial death of JESUS CHRIST. JESUS now symbolizes in the New Covenant, what the curtain represented in the Old Covenant. The rending of the curtain at the exact time of JESUS' death, that is written about by the Apostle Matthew in Matthew 27:51, lets us know that now, only JESUS stands between man and GOD.

Now, only through JESUS, can a person hope to come into the presence of the LIVING GOD in Heaven. HIS death gives believers the much-needed access to GOD that had been missing since the fall of Adam and Eve way back during the infancy of creation. We now have a great HIGH PRIEST in Heaven, WHO, can enable us to enter into the presence of GOD, with pure and true hearts, fully and confidently trusting in HIM. Our evil consciences have been sprinkled by the blood of CHRIST to make us clean, and our bodies have been washed with pure water.

With unwavering confidence, we can hold tightly to the "Christian Hope", and know that GOD can be trusted to keep HIS promise. What we most need to concentrate on now is assembling together, finding ways to encourage each other to love, and seeking to do good deeds for one another whenever possible.

In the New Testament Greek, the word used for "patience" is "hypomeno", and it involves an overcoming of difficulties, and withstanding the pressures of life. It is in fact, a "patient endurance", or, perseverance. In verses 19-39, the author of GOD is calling on us to persevere as we walk in the newness of life that we find in CHRIST JESUS. We must stand strong for CHRIST, and we must also, both, encourage, and warn each other that the second coming of JESUS in drawing near, and will occur unexpectedly.

He also tells us that if we continue on living sinful lives, after we have received the full knowledge of GOD's word, there is no other sacrifice that can be rendered to cover such sins. The defiant sinner has nothing to look forward to, except the sting of GOD's judgment and the terrible, raging fires of hell that will ultimately consume them. For that is the price one must pay for insulting and grieving the HOLY SPIRIT, WHO brings GOD's mercy to HIS people.

We must try and never forget the early days of our Christianity, and how we were determined to remain faithful through the persecutions and pressures of satan, who tried mightily, to get us to turn back to the ways of the world. We must stay focused on GOD, eagerly awaiting the good things that are waiting for us in GOD's promised "Place of Rest", and we must maintain the faith in CHRIST that assures us our salvation through HIM.

WHAT DID WE LEARN FROM CHAPTER TEN?
Here are some key points to remember

(1). The yearly sacrifices, that were performed under the Old Covenant, served only as annual reminders of one's sins. (Hebrews 10:3)

(2). Obedience is better than sacrifice. (Hebrews 10:8-9)

(3). JESUS rendered HIS OWN body as the perfect sacrifice for our sins, once and for all time. (Hebrews 10:12)

(4). JESUS' sacrifice enables all of our sins, past, present, and future, to be forgiven and therefore, there is no need to offer more sacrifices. (Hebrews 10:18)

(5). JESUS is the only way to GOD in Heaven. (Hebrews 10:19-22)

(6). There will be a terrible judgment for professed Christians who deliberately continue to live sinful lives after coming to a full knowledge of the word of GOD. (Hebrews 10:26-27)

(7). Our salvation is assured through our faith in CHRIST. (Hebrews 10:39)

CHAPTER ELEVEN:

(41)

ROLL CALL OF THE FAITHFUL

SCRIPTURE:
The King James Version
Hebrews 11

11 (1) Now faith is the substance of things hoped for, the evidence of things not seen. (2) For by it the elders obtained a good report. (3) Through faith we understand that the worlds were framed by the word of GOD, so that things which are seen were not made of things which do appear. (4) By faith Abel offered unto GOD a more excellent sacrifice than Cain, by which he obtained witness that he was righteous, GOD testifying of his gifts: and by it he being dead yet speaketh. (5) By faith Enoch was translated that he should not see death; and was not found, because GOD had translated him: for before his translation he had this testimony, that he pleased GOD. (6) But without faith it is impossible to please HIM: for he that cometh to GOD must believe that HE is, and that HE is a rewarder of them that diligently seek HIM. (7) By faith Noah, being warned of GOD of things not seen as yet, moved with fear, prepared an ark to the saving of his house; by the which he condemned the world, and became heir of the righteousness which is by faith. (8) By faith Abraham, when he was called to go out into a place which he should after receive for an inheritance, obeyed; and he went out, not knowing whither he went. (9) By faith he sojourned in the land of promise, as in a strange country, dwelling in tabernacles with Isaac and Jacob, the heirs with him of the same promise: (10) For he looked for a city which hath foundations, whose builder and maker is GOD. (11) Through faith also Sara herself received strength to conceive seed, and was delivered of a child when she was past age, because she judged HIM faithful WHO had promised. (12) Therefore sprang there even of one, and him as good as dead, so many as the stars of the sky in multitude, and as the sand which is by the sea shore innumerable. (13) These all died in faith, not having received the promises, but having seen them afar off, and were persuaded of them, and embraced them, and confessed that they were strangers and pilgrims on the earth. (14) For they that say such things declare plainly that they seek a country. (15) And truly, if they had been mindful of that country from whence they came out, they might have had opportunity to have returned. (16) But now they desire a better country, that is, an heavenly: wherefore GOD is not ashamed to be called their GOD: for HE hath prepared for them a city. (17) BY faith Abraham, when he was tried, offered up Isaac: and he that had received the promises offered up his only begotten son, (18) Of whom it was said, "That in Isaac shall thy seed be called:" (19) Accounting that GOD was able to raise him up, even from the dead; from whence also he received him in a figure. (20) By faith Isaac blessed Jacob and Esau concerning things to come.

(21) By faith Jacob, when he was a dying, blessed both the sons of Joseph; and worshipped, leaning upon the top of his staff. (22) By faith Joseph, when he died, made mention of the departing of the children of Israel; and gave commandment concerning his bones. (23) By faith Moses, when he was born, was hid three months of his parents, because they saw he was a proper child; and they were not afraid of the king's commandment. (24) By faith Moses, when he was come to years, refused to be called the son of Pharaoh's daughter; (25) Choosing rather to suffer affliction with the people of GOD, than to enjoy the pleasures of sin for a season; (26) Esteeming the reproach of CHRIST greater riches than the treasures in Egypt: for he had respect unto the recompence of the reward. (27) By faith he forsook Egypt, not fearing the wrath of the king: for he endured, as seeing HIM WHO is invisible. (28) Through faith he kept the Passover, and the sprinkling of blood, lest HE that destroyed the firstborn should touch them. (29) By faith they passed through the Red Sea as by dry land: which the Egyptians assaying to do were drowned. (30) By faith the walls of Jericho fell down, after they were compassed about seven days. (31) By faith the harlot Rahab perished not with them that believed not, when she had received the spies with peace. (32) And what shall I say more? For the time would fail me to tell of Gedeon, and Barak, and of Samson, and of Jephthae; of David also, and Samuel, and of the prophets: (33) Who through faith subdued kingdoms, wrought righteousness, obtained promises, stopped the mouths of lions, (34) Quenched the violence of fire, escaped the edge of the sword, out of weakness were made strong, waxed valiant in fight, turned to flight the armies of the aliens. (35) Women received their dead raised to life again: and others were tortured, not accepting deliverance; that they might obtain a better resurrection: (36) And others had trial of cruel mockings and scourgings, yea, moreover of bonds and imprisonment: (37) They were stoned, they were sawn asunder, were tempted, were slain with the sword: they wandered about in sheepskins and goatskins; being destitute, afflicted, tormented; (38) (Of WHOM the world was not worthy:) they wandered in deserts, and in mountains, and in dens and caves of the earth. (39)

And these all, having obtained a good report through faith, received not the promise: (40) GOD having provided some better things for us, that they without us should not be made perfect.

COMMENTARY:

In the New Testament Greek, the word used for faith is "pistis", and it means "to rely upon with an inward certainty". Faith is being certain of the things we hope for, and being convinced of things we cannot yet see. It is by faith, that we understand that the world was fashioned by the Word of GOD, and that, what is seen, came, from what is not seen. The Christian attitude is that, in terms of eternity, it is better to stake everything on GOD than it is to trust the temporal rewards of this world. It is belief in GOD against the world, the spirit against the senses, and the future against the present.

In Hebrews chapter 11, the author of GOD takes us on a journey back in time with a sort of "roll call", and or, "revisit" with the "who's who" of people who personify "faith" in the Scriptures. He begins with Abel, the second son of Adam and Eve, and the younger brother of Cain, whose story is depicted in Genesis 4:1-8. This story speaks to how we need to respond to GOD in the "right way", because, the way we respond to GOD exemplifies the level of faith we have in HIM, and, the amount of reverence we have for HIM.

Here, we see Abel offering up to GOD, a living sacrifice. It was a sacrifice of living blood, one that symbolizes the giving of one's life to GOD. He responded to GOD in the "right way". Cain, on the other hand, responded by giving GOD the fruit of the ground, something that had been plucked from life, something that was dead. He responded to GOD in the "wrong way".

The writer of Hebrews then directs our attention to Enoch, the father of Methuselah, the man who lived longer than any human in the history of the world, (969 years), and how Enoch lived in close fellowship with GOD all of his life, before being "raptured" up by GOD, before his death. He was 365 years old at that time. He had a "right relationship" of "faith" with GOD, and thus, was rewarded for it.

In Hebrews 11:7, we are reminded of the unconquerable faith of Noah, whose story is told by Moses in Genesis chapters 6-9, and how Noah obeyed GOD when HE instructed him to build the Ark on dry land, nowhere near water, a project that took some 100 years to complete, simply because GOD promised him that HE would send a flood to destroy the earth. Noah's response was one of "total faith" that GOD would do what HE said HE would do. He staked everything on GOD, the future against the presence, and the spirit against the senses.

The author of GOD also recounts the life of the towering figure known as Abraham, the one to whom all Jews trace their origins, and how he was told by GOD to leave his father's house and go into an unknown land that GOD promised him for an inheritance.

He tells of how Abraham and his beautiful wife Sarah had faith, even in their old age, that GOD would deliver unto them a son who would be, just the beginning, of a whole race of people who would become HIS "chosen" nation (Israel). They relied on GOD with an "inward certainty", and were convinced of the things GOD promised, that they could not yet see. They were willing to venture into the unknown, because they felt secure with GOD's promise.

The writer goes on to tell the familiar stories of the faith of Joseph, Jacob, Moses, Rahab and the likes. These were people who never actually got to see the end result of all the things that GOD had promised, however, the blessings of GOD have no ending, and extend well beyond the life expectancy of any man or woman. HIS blessings were extended to their families for generations to come, and through their faith and hope, they could see it all from a distance.

When we come into a "right relationship" with GOD, as these people did, GOD allows us to see, from way on high, our lives, from HIS lofty and majestic point of view. All of these people received GOD's approval, and were counted righteous, because of their faith. Yet, none of them received all the things that GOD had promised, during their earthly lifetimes, because you can only receive the eternal things, the prize at the end of the race, after the race itself is finished.

Faith is what orients a person to GOD. When stripped down to its most basic form, it is simply the confidence and belief we have that GOD really exists. And those, who possess such a confidence in GOD, also share a conviction in knowing that GOD will reward them because they earnestly seek after HIM with their whole hearts (minds).

The people of faith, who are mentioned in Hebrews 11, when compared to the modern-day believer, had relatively little knowledge of GOD, and, they did not get to hear the wisdom of JESUS' words the way we have in this day. How much more motivated to have faith in the ONLY WISE GOD we should be! And because we know JESUS, from a Monday morning quarterback's perspective, we should be able to easily live a life of faith and obedience to GOD, because of HIS faithfulness and goodness to us, throughout the course of time.

WHAT DID WE LEARN FROM CHAPTER ELEVEN?
Here are some key points to remember

(1). Faith is the confident assurance that what we hope for is going to happen. (Hebrews 11:1)

(2). Faith is the key that opens up the doors to Heaven. (Hebrews 11)

(3). The entire universe was spoken into existence by GOD. (Hebrews 11:3)

(4). All of the people mentioned in chapter 11 received salvation before there was a Ten Commandments, and so the key to receiving salvation rests in our faith in GOD, and JESUS CHRIST, and not, on what we can do for ourselves. (Hebrews 11:39)

(5). A person of faith has the courage to trust GOD all the way unto death. (Hebrews 11:32-38)

CHAPTER TWELVE:

FAITHFULNESS AND DISCIPLINE

SCRIPTURE:
The King James Version
Hebrews 12:1-13

(12) (1) Wherefore seeing we also are compassed about with so great a cloud of witnesses, let us lay aside every weight, and the sin which doth so easily beset us, and let us run with patience the race that is set before us. (2) Looking unto JESUS the AUTHOR and FINISHER of our faith; WHO for the joy that was set before HIM endured the cross, despising the shame, and is set down at the right hand of the throne of GOD. (3) For consider HIM that endured such contradiction of sinners against HIMSELF, lest ye be wearied and faint in your minds. (4) Ye have not yet resisted unto blood, striving against sin. (5) And ye have forgotten the exhortation which speaketh unto you as unto children, "MY son, despise not thou the chastening of the LORD, nor faint when thou art rebuked of HIM: (6) For whom the LORD loveth HE chasteneth, and scourgeth every son whom HE receiveth." (7) If ye endure chastening, GOD dealeth with you as with sons; for what son is he whom the father chasteneth not? (8) But if ye be without chastisement, whereof all are partakers, then are ye bastards, and not sons. (9) Furthermore we have had fathers of our flesh which corrected us, and we gave them reverence: shall we not much rather be in subjection unto the FATHER of spirits, and live? (10) For they verily for a few days chastened us after their own pleasure; but HE for our profit, that we might be partakers of HIS holiness. (11) Now no chastening for the present seemeth to be joyous, but grievous: nevertheless afterward it yieldeth the peaceable fruit of righteousness unto them which are exercised thereby. (12) Wherefore lift up the hands which hang down, and the feeble knees; (13) And make straight paths for your feet, lest that which is lame be turned out of the way; but let it rather be healed.

COMMENTARY:

In Hebrews chapter 12, the author of GOD gives us a remarkably vivid description and summary of the Christian life, and, shows us the attitude we should have, as we aspire to obtain our goal of becoming more like CHRIST. In the Greek, the word used for "discipline" is "paideia" (pahee-di-ah), and it is "education or training". It also means "to nurture, instruct, or chasten".

The Christian life can be likened to a relay race. The people of faith, like the ones mentioned in Hebrews chapter 11, who have run before us, have passed on the baton, and now, they anxiously wait to see how we will carry on in the discipline that Christianity demands. As we run, we can look back and see how JESUS ran HIS race, and, at one and the same time, we can also look ahead, and see HIS exaltation at the finish line.

JESUS, is our supreme example, and, HE is the "Author and Finisher" of our faith (Hebrews 12:1-2). A life that is void of testing from GOD is most likely going to be a life void of prayer, humility, holiness, and appreciation of what GOD has done for us. Tests from GOD are not made to make us fail, but rather, are made to make us better representatives of CHRIST, and Christianity, here on earth.

Trials are what GOD uses to refine us, and prepare us for a life of eternity with HIM, in HIS kingdom. It takes a certain amount of discipline to become, and remain successful in the Christian race. When we take into account how much JESUS endured, we can realize that suffering and hardship are no excuse for us to give up and drop out of contention (Hebrews 12:3-15).

If we fail to understand the love and purpose of GOD's discipline, we are likely to become bitter, and miss out on GOD's graceful intent. If we see our trials and difficulties in the perspective provided by GOD's grace, we will be better able to understand and accept HIS discipline in our lives. Remember, Esau, who saw no value in spiritual things, ended up selling his birthright to GOD's covenant promise, for a mere a bowl of stew. If we value only material things as he did, we too, are in danger of missing our blessings in the end (Hebrews 12:16-17).

We, as Christians, are not people who meander along the paths of life in a totally oblivious manner. We are not like tourist, who, each night, return to the point where we started that previous morning. The Christian life is about going somewhere, and at the end of each day, we'll do good to ask ourselves, "Have we gotten any closer to our goal of being more like CHRIST?" That should be the aspiration of every Christian, to, each day, become more and more like CHRIST.

However, the Christian also has another inspiration. It is the inspiration of the "cloud of witnesses", who have gone before us, and witnessed their confession to CHRIST, and now witness our performance from way on high. They are those people mentioned in Hebrews chapter 11, who personified faith during their Christian walk here on earth. They are those people like Moses, Abraham, and Noah, who have already claimed their crowns of victory.

But, unfortunately, we Christians also have "a handicap", and it is "the handicap and weight of our own sins". It is very difficult to run a race, when you are carrying excess baggage. If we wish to travel far, it is much better to travel light. The burden of sin can weigh heavily on a person, who is trying to run the Christian race, or walk the Christian walk. It is paramount that we first discard the unnecessary things that hold us back, and what holds man back is sin. If we are to endure the Christian race to the finish, we must first learn to lighten our load of "sinful cargo" (behavior), and move away from our carnal desires (sin nature) (Hebrews 12:1).

Our supreme example of faith and discipline is CHRIST JESUS HIMSELF. HE is also our companion along the way, and, HE is our goal at the end of the race. Remember, GOD's kingdom will remain when the universe itself is shaken, and this old world itself will ultimately disappear. That is when one will truly appreciate how good it will be to be a citizen in the kingdom of Heaven. We should also remember that our trials, can and will, both refine us, and, help prepare us to dwell in eternity in the presence of THE ALMIGHTY GOD in Heaven, at the end of our Christian race.

A CALL TO LISTEN TO GOD
Hebrews 12:14-29

12 (14) Follow peace with all men, and holiness, without which no man shall see the LORD: (15) Looking diligently lest any man fail of the grace of GOD; lest any root of bitterness springing up trouble you, and thereby many be defiled; (16) Lest there be any fornicators, or profane person, as Esau, who for one morsel of meat sold his birthright. (17) For ye know how that afterward, when he would have inherited the blessing, he was rejected: for he found no place of repentance, though he sought it carefully with tears. (18) For ye are not come unto the mount that might be touched, and that burned with fire, nor unto blackness, and darkness, and tempest, (19) And the sound of a trumpet, and the voice of words; which voice they that heard intreated that the word should not be spoken to them anymore: (20) (For they could not endure that which was commanded, "And if so much as a beast touch the mountain, it shall be stoned, or thrust through with a dart:" (21) And so terrible was the sight, that Moses said, "I exceedingly fear and quake:)" (22) But ye are come unto mount Sion, and unto the city of the living GOD, the heavenly Jerusalem, and to an innumerable company of angels, (23) To the general assembly and church of the firstborn, which are written in Heaven, and to GOD the JUDGE of all, and to the spirits of just men made perfect, (24) And to JESUS the MEDIATOR of the New Covenant, and to the blood of sprinkling, that speaketh better things than that of Abel. (25) See that ye refuse not HIM that speaketh. For if they escaped not who refused him that spake on earth, much more shall not we escape, if we turn away from HIM that speaketh from Heaven: (26) WHOSE voice then shook the earth: but now HE hath promised, saying, "Yet once more I shake not the earth only, but also Heaven." (27) And this word, "Yet once more", signifieth the removing of those things that are shaken, as of things that are made, that those things which cannot be shaken may remain. (28) Wherefore we receiving a kingdom which cannot be moved, let us have grace, whereby we may serve GOD acceptably with reverence and GODly fear: (29) For our GOD is a consuming fire.

COMMENTARY:

The motivation for pursuing holiness here and now, is the realization that, without it, no one can see GOD, or stand in the presence of GOD in the spiritual life that follows our stay here on earth. In other words, Christians must be, and will be, sinless when they see the LORD in Heaven.

A person's perception of GOD in this present life is the true measure of his or her holiness. In order to help us reach the state of holiness we need to achieve, GOD whips us into condition with his Holy discipline, and testing. When we fail to understand the love and purpose of GOD's discipline, we are likely to become bitter towards HIM, and thereby, miss HIS unfailing grace. However, when we are able to see our trials and difficulties in the perspective of GOD's grace, we are better able to accept HIS chastening.

In Hebrews 12:14-29, the author calls for a renewed spiritual vitality among GOD's people. It is a call to listen to GOD with a renewed interest in how HE wants us to live our lives here on earth. He also urges us to begin by trying to live in peace with one another, being a good example for those who have not yet reached your own stage of spiritual awareness, so that not even one of us will miss out on GOD's special favor.

We can also help others guard against going astray by being accountable to one another, making sure that the bitter root of immorality does not infiltrate the lives of ourselves, and, of those whom we are close to. Beginning in verse 18, the author of Hebrews gives us a final warning, as he vividly depicts with his writing, a clear picture of the situation on Mount Sinai, where the Old Covenant was given to the people in an awesome way that only GOD could stage.

Here he describes the scene of that event as a place of flaming fire, darkness and gloom, and a whirlwind, as GOD delivered HIS laws to the Israelites. And they could hear an awesome trumpet blast accompanied by a voice with a message so terrible that they begged GOD to stop speaking. Even Moses was admittedly terrified by this awesome display of GOD's power.

However, in verse 22, the writer reminds the people that, that was then, and this is now. Now we fall under the protection of the New Covenant, which was ushered in by CHRIST JESUS, and the realities pertained to in it are even more impressive because they are Heavenly, and not only is there a Heavenly city, but there is also, both, angels, and, the spirits of those who have been redeemed and made perfect by the LORD.

Ultimately, all created things will be removed by GOD. When Moses gave the law at the foot of Mount Sinai, the mountain itself burned with fire, and the surrounding plains shook uncontrollably. The fear that was felt by those who were present at that event will be nothing compared to what will be felt by those who cannot see spiritual realities through faith, and as a result, fail to enter into the Kingdom of Heaven.

The Kingdom of Heaven is all that will remain after the universe itself is shaken apart, and all of creation disappears. We must see to it that we obey GOD, the ONE WHO is speaking to us. If the people of Israel didn't escape the wrath of GOD when they refused to listen to Moses, GOD's earthly messenger, then, how much more terrible it will be for those of us, in this day, who refuse to listen to CHRIST JESUS, WHO came directly from Heaven to warn us.

And since GOD, through HIS tender mercies, has given us a choice to be redeemed, and spend eternity with HIM in Heaven, let us be thankful and begin worshipping

HIM in spirit, and, in truth, with holy fear and reverence, because our GOD is truly a consuming fire.

WHAT DID WE LEARN FROM CHAPTER TWELVE?
Here are some key points to remember

(1). Sin is a weight that slows us down in our Christian walk, and hinders our spiritual progress toward the LORD. (Hebrews 12:1a)

(2). Our spiritual walk can be likened to an endurance race, which GOD HIMSELF, has placed before us to run. (Hebrews 12:1b)

(3). JESUS HIMSELF is the great example as to how we should run our Christian race. (Hebrews 12:2)

(4). JESUS is also the inspiration we need in order to endure our grueling race, and, is also, the prize that awaits us at the finish line. (Hebrews 12:2-4)

(5). GOD disciplines us all along the way, in order to strengthen us, and, enable us to reach our goal. (Hebrews 12:5-13)

(6). Without holiness, no one can see GOD. (Hebrews 12:14)

(7). We must help each other guard against going astray to sin. (Hebrews 12:15)

(8). If we obey GOD, our prize will be a Kingdom that cannot be destroyed. (Hebrews 12:25-28)

CHAPTER THIRTEEN:

LOOKING OUT FOR OTHERS

SCRIPTURE:
The King James Version
Hebrews 13

13 (1) Let brotherly love continue. (2) Be not forgetful to entertain strangers: for thereby some have entertained angels unawares. (3) Remember them that are in bonds, as bound with them: and them which suffer adversity, as being yourselves also in the body. (4) Marriage is honourable in all, and the bed undefiled: but whoremongers and adulterers GOD will judge. (5) Let your conversation be without covetousness; and be content with such things as ye have: for HE hath said, "I will never leave thee, nor forsake thee", (6) So that we may boldly say, "The LORD is my helper, and I will not fear what man shall do unto me". (7) Remember them which have the rule over you, who have spoken unto you the word of GOD: whose faith follow, considering the end of their conversation. (8) JESUS CHRIST the same yesterday, and today, and forever. (9) Be not carried about with divers and strange doctrines. For it is a good thing that the heart be established with grace; not with meats, which have not profited them that have been occupied therein. (10) We have an altar, whereof they have no right to eat which serve the tabernacle. (11) For the bodies of those beasts, whose blood is brought into the sanctuary by the high priest for sin, are burned without the camp. (12) Wherefore JESUS also, that HE might sanctify the people with HIS OWN blood, suffered without the gate. (13) Let us go forth therefore unto HIM without the camp, bearing HIS reproach. (14) For here have we no continuing city, but we seek one to come. (15) By HIM therefore let us offer the sacrifice of praise to GOD continually, that is, the fruit of our lips giving thanks to HIS name. (16) But to do good and to communicate forget not: for with such sacrifices GOD is well pleased. (17) Obey them that have the rule over you, and submit yourselves: for they watch for your souls, as they that must give account, that they may do it with joy, and not with grief: for that is unprofitable for you. (18) Pray for us: for we trust we have a good conscience, in all things willing to live honestly. (19) But I beseech you the rather to do this, that I may be restored to you the sooner. (20) Now the GOD of peace, that brought again from the dead our LORD JESUS, that GREAT SHEPHERD of the sheep, through the blood of the everlasting covenant, (21) Make you perfect in every good work to do HIS will, working in you that which is well pleasing in HIS sight, through JESUS CHRIST; to WHOM be glory for ever and ever. Amen. (22) And I beseech you, brethren, suffer the word of exaltation: for I have written a letter unto you in few words. (23) Know ye that our brother Timothy is set at liberty; with whom, if he come shortly, I will see you. (24) Salute all them that have the rule over you, and all the saints. They of Italy salute you. (25) Grace be with you all. Amen.

COMMENTARY:

The book of Hebrews concludes with a series of exhortations to Christians, and indeed, to all mankind, concerning how we should live a life of faith, here on earth. We are called to love and trust in GOD, and to continue to listen to, and respect those leaders who first introduced us to the LORD.

Here believers are called to live a life of love for their fellowman (verse 1). Christians should not forget to show hospitality to everyone, because you never know when you might be entertaining an angel (verse 2). We should even remember and pray for the freedom of those who have been incarcerated because of their zeal and work for CHRIST, with the same passion and frequency with which we pray for ourselves. And finally, we must bear each other's burdens, as so to fulfill the command of CHRIST JESUS.

The epilogue of this letter to the Hebrews is distinguished from its body, in that, it contains specific admonitions that we should adhere to. It contains not only the writer's personal comments, but also gives specific instructions suggesting how we can worship GOD in a more acceptable manner than we've become accustomed to.

Verses 1-6 contains moral directions for us to follow, that would reflects our personal kindness to our brothers, to strangers, and, to those who are imprisoned. This passage also calls for sexual purity in marriage, and, for us to avoid monetary greed, being content with what the LORD is blessing each of us with, personally.

Even if we have little on the material level, we still have GOD's daily help, just as HE promises us.

These moral instructions are followed by some religious directions in verses 7-17. Here the writer reminds us that we are to not forget those religious leaders who first taught us the word of GOD, and, we are to always remember and consider all of the good that has come to us from their lives, and then finally, we are to trust GOD just as they do.

CHRIST JESUS is the same, yesterday, today, and forever, and we should not be distracted by any other strange, new ideology, or theology that comes down the pike. JESUS affords us with an altar from which no earthly priest can eat, and then, HE died outside the gates of Jerusalem to make us holy by the shedding of HIS OWN blood. HE was then raised from the dead by GOD the FATHER, so that HE could carry HIS OWN blood back to the Temple in Heaven, and then offer it, as a sacrificial payment for our sins.

We must therefore go out and be willing to suffer the same kind of disgrace and persecution that JESUS suffered for us, in route to, and on, the cross at Golgotha. The apostle John wrote in his third letter, which was a personal note to his friend Gaius, that, "I have no greater joy than this, to hear that my children are walking in the truth" (3 John 4).

In Hebrews 13:17-19, the author of GOD lays down the duty and responsibility of the Christian congregation to its leaders, whom GOD has chosen. Obedience to its leaders is a duty of the congregation. And while a Christian church is a democracy, it is not a democracy that is taken to extremes. Obedience is not given to its leaders in order to gratify their sense of power and prestige, but rather, it is given so that, we who trust in GOD, can allow them to shepherd and care for those souls which GOD has appointed to them.

A true man of GOD recognizes his responsibility to GOD, and is accountable for his actions, right or wrong. Our obedience to our leaders is not a blind one however, and nor is it a surrender of our responsibility to obey CHRIST as LORD of the Church. We must, however, remain responsive to those, whom GOD has given us as guides, and allow ourselves to be influenced positively by them. Our getting to know GOD personally through HIS word gives us the ability to distinguish true men of GOD from those who are frauds.

Looking out for each other entails watching out and praying for others in the congregation in general, as well as for those on the leadership tier in the Church. In the spiritual sense, we truly are our brother's keeper, and we are called to help each other guard against going astray. It is appropriate that leaders are called to watch over us, and, in the end, they must give an account to GOD, regarding how they fared as shepherds. But, in the same way, we are called to watch over each other, and, must also give an account to GOD, for our reactions concerning the needs of our fellowman, especially within the Church.

WHAT DID WE LEARN FROM CHAPTER THIRTEEN?
Here are some key points to remember

(1). We must not only love one another as Christians, but we must also show hospitality to strangers. (Hebrews 13:1-2)

(2). We must have compassion for those who are imprisoned, and, for those people who are mistreated. (Hebrews 13:3)

(3). Do not commit adultery. (Hebrews 13:4)

(4). Do not fall in love with money and material things. (Hebrews 13:5)

(5). Respect the teachers of GOD's word, and trust in GOD as they do. (Hebrews 13:7)

(6). JESUS CHRIST is unchangeable. (Hebrews 13:8)

(7). We must praise GOD with our lips. Hebrews 13:15)

(8). Obey those spiritual leaders whom you know are following the word of GOD. (Hebrews 13:17)

(9). We must pray for our spiritual leaders. (Hebrews 13:18-19)

(55)

BONUS SECTION:

ADHERENTS

Of

THE WAY

THE TRUTH

AND

THE LIFE

A LOOK INTO THE LIVES OF JESUS' ORIGINAL HAND-PICKED DISCIPLES (Including the Apostle Paul)

INTRODUCTION:

THE WAY, THE TRUTH, AND THE LIFE

In the beginning GOD created the heaven and the earth. In the beginning was the WORD, and the WORD was with GOD, and the WORD was GOD. All things were made by HIM, and without HIM, was not any thing made, that was made. In HIM was life, and the LIFE was the LIGHT of men. At that time, the earth was without form, and void, and darkness was upon the face of the deep. And the HOLY SPIRIT of GOD moved upon the face of the waters. And GOD said, "Let there be LIGHT" and there was LIGHT. And the LIGHT shined in the darkness; and the darkness can never extinguish IT.

And so, JESUS was in the world, and, the world was made by HIM, but the world, still, does not know HIM. HE was made flesh, born of woman, so that HE could dwell among humankind. HE showed HIMSELF to be full of unfailing love and faithfulness. And some were blessed enough to see HIS glory, and we have all, of course, benefited from the richness of HIS sacrifice, one gracious blessing after another.

HE first came to HIS OWN chosen people, and HIS OWN chosen people rejected HIM. However, to all those that do believe in HIM, and accept HIM, to them, HE gives the power to become "Children of GOD". Because of our belief in CHRIST JESUS, we are "born again", not through a physical birth that is a result of human passion or plan, but rather, it is a rebirth that comes spiritually from GOD. The Law was given to us through Moses, but GOD's unfailing love and faithfulness, comes to us through CHRIST JESUS.

GOD has already placed within us, seven communicable attributes, which make it possible for us to share HIS nature, worship HIM, and have a personal relationship with HIM, through CHRIST JESUS. Those attributes include Life, personality, love, truth, wisdom, justice, and holiness. In addition, GOD gives us CHRIST JESUS, and the HOLY SPIRIT, so that we will be able to see exactly what HE is like, and only JESUS, can usher us into GOD's OWN glorious presence, without fear, guilt, or shame. If we desire to end up in GOD's presence, we must choose CHRIST, and become "adherents of HIS way".

The HOLY SPIRIT and the Bride (The Christian Church) say come, but the lure of this world and satan say the same. As Christians, the HOLY SPIRIT in us will always compel us towards CHRIST, however, the "sin nature" in us, will always try and tug us back, toward the world. That battle within us, between the REASON to do right" (The HOLY SPIRIT) and the "Passion to want to do wrong" (Sin Nature) stays with us, long after we accept the gift of Salvation. However, through our strength in CHRIST, we can "overcome" the gravitational pull of this world, just as CHRIST did, and find ourselves in the "ultimate happy ending", that has been prepared for us, by GOD, from the very foundation of this world.

WHAT IS "THE WAY"?

The term "The Way" is what JESUS' teachings and doctrine were called before the terms "Christianity", or "Christian" came about. JESUS' followers were originally called "Adherents of the Way". It was not until the first Gentile church of The Way was formed in Antioch of Syria by some of the Believers who had fled Jerusalem to find safety from persecution, following the death of Stephen (Acts 11:26), that, the term "Christian" was first used.

When the Church at Jerusalem heard about how "The Way" was being effectively preached to the Gentiles at Antioch, they sent Barnabas there to bring back a report. Encouraged by what he saw, Barnabas urged the new believers to stay true to The Way, or, the doctrine of CHRIST.

Barnabas later went to Tarsus, the hometown of the apostle Paul, and brought him back to Antioch to help preach the gospel for an entire year to the newly founded "Christian Church". This all happened about nine years after Paul had been run out of Jerusalem by Greek-speaking Jews who were plotting to murder him (Acts 9:29-30).

At that time, some of the Jews were still afraid of Paul, because, prior to his "Damascus Road conversion" by CHRIST, he had a very well known reputation for killing and persecuting those Jews, who were followers of The Way (Acts 9:1-28). In fact, Paul was there in Jerusalem, urging those men on, who were stoning GOD's servant, Stephen, to death (Acts 7:58).

However, when Barnabas first introduced Paul to the Church at Jerusalem, all of the apostles believed his conversion story (Acts 9:27-28)) and accepted him and allowed him to remain with them and preach the gospel to the believers there, until he was forced to leave by those hostile Hellenistic Jews that I mentioned earlier.

Soon Paul, Barnabas, John Mark, Luke, Silas, and many other believers would take their show on the road, and "The Way of CHRIST" would be preached and spread to the far corners of the earth with explosive power and determination. And those, now famous, missionary journeys would catapult this little known sect of The Way, into one of the most powerful religious influences in the world, by the end of the first century.

In Matthew chapter 7, verses 24-29, JESUS concluded HIS, now famous, "Sermon on the Mount" with this warning for us to build our foundations on the "Most High Faith". There, we see JESUS demanding two things. First, HE demands that we "Listen", because the first step, toward living a Christian life, calls for us to give JESUS a chance to be heard.

Secondly, JESUS demands that we "do". Knowledge is never relevant, until it is put into action. Knowledge must become action, just as theory must become practice, before theology can become life. There is not much point in going to see an expert, if you are not prepared to act upon his advice.

Millions of Christians go to church every weekend to listen to the teachings of JESUS, and some, as a result, have very good knowledge of what those teachings say. Yet, time and time again, they walk out of the doors of the church house, and fail to put what they've learned into action. If we are in any sense, to become followers of CHRIST, or, Adherents of the Way, we must learn to, first, "Hear", and then, "Do".

There is only one word that sums up "Hearing and Doing", in both the English, and the Greek. In the Greek, that word is "Hupakoe" (Hoop-ak-o-ay), and it means, "to listen attentively, and to heed, or conform, to command or authority". In English, that word is "obedience".

It is JESUS' claim that, obedience to HIM is the only true foundation. "I AM the WAY, the TRUTH, and the LIFE" is what JESUS said to a doubting Thomas in John 14:6. And, in the final analysis, all man ever really seeks is life. He never seeks knowledge, just for knowledge sake, but rather, for what that knowledge can do to make his life more worth living. It is JESUS' contention, that, life through HIM, is, the only life worth living.

No one goes to the FATHER, but by JESUS, because, HE alone, is the WAY to GOD. In HIM, we see exactly what GOD is like, and only HE, can usher us into GOD's OWN glorious presence, without fear, guilt, or shame. JESUS truly is "THE WAY" to go.

THE TEN COMMANDMENTS: THE WAY TO LIVE LIFE ON EARTH

What do we need to hear? In Exodus 20:1-17, GOD HIMSELF gives these instructions to HIS servant Moses on Mount Sinai to take back to those who wish to worship and follow HIM, in spirit, and in truth. The following is the King James Version account of those instructions, which have come to be known as "The Law", or, "The Ten Commandments, and by some scholars they are often referred to as the "Decalogue, from the Greek word meaning "ten words":

Exodus 20:1-17 (KJV)

20 (1) And GOD spake all these words, saying, (2) I AM the LORD thy GOD, which have brought thee out of the land of Egypt, out of the house of bondage. (3) *Thou shalt have no other gods before ME.* (4) *Thou shalt not make unto thee any graven image, or any likeness of any thing that is in heaven above, or that is in the earth beneath, or that is in the water under the earth:* (5) Thou shalt not bow down thyself to them, nor serve them: for I the LORD thy GOD am a jealous GOD, visiting the iniquity of the fathers upon the children unto the third and fourth generation of them that hate ME; (6) And shewing mercy unto thousands of them that love ME, and keep MY commandments. (7) *Thou shalt not take the name of the LORD thy GOD in vain.* (8) *Remember the Sabbath day, to keep it holy.* (9) Six days shalt thou labour, and do all thy work: (10) But the seventh day is the Sabbath of the LORD thy GOD: in it thou shalt not do any work, thou, nor thy son, nor thy daughter, thy manservant, nor thy maidservant, nor thy cattle, nor thy stranger that is within thy gates: (11) For six days the LORD made heaven and earth, the sea, and all that in them is, and rested the seventh day: wherefore the LORD blessed the Sabbath day, and hallowed it. (12) *Honour thy father and thy mother:* that thy days may be long upon the land which the LORD thy GOD giveth thee. (13) *Thou shalt not kill.* (14) *Thou shalt not commit adultery.* (15) *Thou shalt not steal.* (16) *Thou shalt not bear false witness against thy neighbour.* (17) *Thou shalt not covet thy neighbour's house, thou shalt not covet thy neighbour's wife, nor his manservant, nor his maidservant, nor his ox, nor his ass, nor any thing that is thy neighbour's.*

These ten laws, were given by GOD, to Moses, for him to present to us, as a guideline for daily living, and also to show us how far we were from the standard of living that HE originally intended for us. They are to be The Way, by which we should live. They are a part of the covenant between GOD and those of us, who choose to follow HIM, in HIS Way, not our way. These laws have an abiding significance for GOD's character, which never changes. They originate from HIM and HIS eternal character and their moral value cannot be changed.

Some 1300 years after GOD gave man these laws, HE sent HIS only begotten SON, JESUS, to clarify and uphold them. JESUS did not come to cancel them, nor did HE come to alter them. In fact, HE actually placed these laws on a higher plane, by demanding that the spiritual, as well as the legal aspects of the law be kept. In Matthew 5:17-19, JESUS put HIS OWN eternal stamp on the Decalogue, by declaring, "Do not think I came to destroy the Law or the Prophets, I did not come to destroy but to fulfill".

The Ten Commandments form the heart of the special covenant between GOD and HIS people, but they were never intended to be a set of rules and regulations by which we could earn our salvation. However, the world needs desperately to see the character, and the name of GOD displayed, in the lives of all those Christians, who still take GOD's word seriously. These commandments coupled with the teachings of CHRIST JESUS, are still the best guidelines for practical daily living known to man, anywhere in the world.

In Matthew 22:34-40, an expert in religious law stood up to test JESUS by asking HIM which is the first, most important, or, greatest of the Ten Commandments, that were delivered by Moses. JESUS replied that, "You must love the LORD your GOD with all of your heart, all of your soul, and all of your mind. This is the first and greatest commandment". This statement by JESUS actually encompasses the first four commandments. In order for a person to abide by that statement, "Love the LORD your GOD with all of your heart, soul, and mind", one would have to also adhere to obeying the first four commandments.

In the second part of JESUS' answer to the religious scholar, HE says, "And a second is equally important: Love your neighbor as yourself". This statement encompasses the last six commandments. In order for a person to adhere to and obey the second part of JESUS' statement, "Love your neighbor as yourself", a person would have to adhere to, and obey, those last six commandments.

That is why JESUS concludes HIS answer by stating, that, "All the other commandments, and all the demands of the prophets are based on these two commandments". If a person adheres to those two commandments, he or she will automatically adhere to the Decalogue. And if a person's heart is fixed on GOD, he or she will have the right attitude toward others. The right motive, which is pleasing GOD, WHO is first in our life, will automatically result in obeying the other commandments. Consequently, the desires that emanate out of the hearts of men will never intentionally cause pain, or loss, to others.

JESUS greatly enlarged on the meaning and intent of the Ten Commandments by emphasizing the "heart attitude", and the Christian receives a blessed joy on earth, whenever we decide to set our priorities straight with GOD. All of these commandments represent the guideline, or The Way, by which we should live life on earth, but CHRIST JESUS still represents the only Way to eternal life, a path that can only come through our acceptance of, and our belief in HIM. And just as the only way back to glory for JESUS was, through the cross, so it is, with those of us who follow HIM.

THE AFFIRMATION OF JESUS ON THE HEARTS OF MEN

In Mark chapter 8, verses 27-29, John Mark writes of the 25-mile walk, of JESUS and HIS Disciples, from Galilee to Caesarea-Philippi. Now it is no accident that JESUS chose this particular time and area to pose these questions to HIS Disciples, "Who do men say that I AM?" And subsequently, "Who do you say that I AM"?

At that time, Caesarea-Philippi was notorious for "idol worship". In fact, it was an olio of various religions. There were no less than fourteen temples of idol worship in the immediate vicinity of Caesarea-Philippi. First of all, the Syrian Gods were worshipped there.

There was also a mountain in Caesarea-Philippi with a deep cavern that was said to be the birthplace of "Pan", the Greek God of Nature. In fact, Pan was the source of Caesarea-Philippi's former name of, "Paneas", which was changed by Herod the Great's son, Philip the Tetrarch, in honor of Caesar Augustus. Herod the Great himself had also constructed a huge white marble tower, the most imposing edifice in Caesarea-Philippi at that time, and dedicated it too, to Caesar Augustus, who was also worshipped as a God.

Caesarea-Philippi is also the place where the Jordan River begins. We all know the Jordan River as the place where John the Baptist did most of his baptizing. In fact, it was there where he baptized his cousin, JESUS, at the beginning of HIS three-year ministry

And so, it is against this backdrop of Greek and Syrian gods, and also a place where some of the history of Israel itself can be found, that, we see this carpenter's SON from Nazareth, stand and pose the question to HIS disciples, "Who do men say that I am?

Here JESUS deliberately sets HIMSELF against the backdrop of the world's religions of the day, in the midst of all of their history and splendor, and softly demands to be compared to them, and fully expect the verdict to be rendered in HIS favor! Nowhere else in scripture does JESUS' awareness of HIS OWN deity seem to come through to us in a more clear and precise way.

In the Greek, the word used for "affirmation" is "bebaiosis" (beb-ah-yo-sis), and it means, "to be steadfast and sure in one's assertions". When Peter pondered this question from JESUS, he knew that all human categories had already failed to describe just WHO JESUS really was. This passage, perhaps, serves to show us, that, our discovery of JESUS must be a personal discovery, because here we see JESUS also asks the question, "Who do "you" say that I AM?

Our knowledge of JESUS must never be "secondhand". Christianity does not consist of knowing about JESUS, but rather, it consists of knowing JESUS "firsthand". Our LORD and SAVIOR, always demands, a personal verdict from each of us. When JESUS asked this question, HE was not just asking it to HIS original Disciples. It is also a question that is directed to us, from across the spans of time, in hopes that we too can answer it favorably and know in our hearts that JESUS is not only "the only way to GOD", but is also, "ONE with GOD".

JESUS' Transfiguration (Mark 9:1-10), which in all geographical likelihood, occurred on Mount Hermon nearly 2000 years ago, was meant to place "affirmation" of JESUS' majesty, on the hearts of all men. GOD spoke from the clouds that day to Peter, James, and John, to forever "affirm" in their hearts, that JESUS truly is HIS only begotten SON. And HE used the images of Moses and Elijah, "the Law" and "the Prophet", two towering figures in Jewish history, both of whom, no man had seen die. But they were there, never the less, to help bring "affirmation" to this divine event.

And, as for Peter, James and John, they, in a very special sense, had become witnesses to the glory of CHRIST. And now, they had the story of that glory embedded in their hearts, so that they may go out and tell all men that JESUS truly is the SON of the living GOD.

We may never be able to witness an event, such as the "Transfiguration of CHRIST", that occurred on a mountaintop overlooking Caesarea-Philippi that day.

But certainly, we can all follow the instructions of JESUS, as they were handed down to Peter and the Disciples from a mountain in Galilee, on a separate occasion, that is recorded in Matthew 28:19-20 (The Great Commission).

Each of us can go out and witness to everyone we meet on a day to day basis, about the wonderful Gospel of JESUS CHRIST, offering to all those who will listen, the saving knowledge of the Word of GOD. We are, just like the original disciples, instructed by JESUS to go out and teach men, to teach men, to teach men, to teach men.... For all time, always remembering that we too, are indeed, "Adherents of the Way", and that JESUS is indeed, the ONLY WAY to eternal life in Heaven.

And now, in the following pages, we will delve, as deeply as we can, into the lives of the original "Adherents of the Way", who worked diligently in the first century, to help establish and develop the early Christian Church during its infancy.

THE APOSTLE PETER

William E. Channing wrote in his essay, "Means of promoting Christianity", that, "The first laborers do little more than teach those who come after them, what to avoid, and how to labor more effectually than themselves".

The "Christian Hope" has, throughout the history of the Church, served as motivation to make life on earth conform more fully to the word of GOD, just as it was presented to us by JESUS CHRIST, during HIS three-year ministry. All the information we have about CHRIST comes to us from those who actually saw HIS miracles performed, and actually heard HIM speak. But, because they wrote to encourage believers, rather than to satisfy historical curiosity, this information, often leave more questions, than it does answers, particularly, in the minds of the unbeliever.

No one has ever been able to harmonize all of this information into a completely satisfying chronological account. These Holy Scriptures, as we see them, where not assembled by the authors of GOD who wrote them, but rather, they were assembled much later on, by second, third, and even fourth generation workers of the early church.

It must not be forgotten, however, that the original workers of the early church, where those handpicked apostles of JESUS CHRIST. One man emerged as the leader of that band of men and his name was Peter. New Testament writers use four different names in referring to Peter. They are "Simeon" (Acts 15:14), which means "hearing", "Simon", which is the Greek form of "Simeon", "Cephas", which is Aramaic for "Rock", and, of course, "Peter", which is Greek for "Rock". Peter was first introduced to JESUS by his brother Andrew (John 1:40-42). When JESUS first met Peter, HE said, "Thou art Simon, the son of Jonas: thou shalt be called Cephas" (John 1:42).

Peter spoke with a Galilean accent and his mannerisms identified him as an uncouth native of the Galilean frontier (cf. Mark 14:70). He is at the top the list of the apostles in all of the gospel accounts, which tends to suggest that New Testament writers considered him to be the most significant of the original twelve disciples.

And, even though, he did not write as much as John or Matthew, he, nevertheless, emerged as the most influential leader in the early church. On the day of the original Pentecost, Peter preached the first sermon ever preached in a Christian Church. And he, along with the apostle John, were the first disciples to perform a miracle, after the Pentecost, when they did so, by healing the cripple man at the gate called beautiful (Acts 3:1-11).

The Roman Catholic Church traces the authority of the Pope back to Peter. It is alleged that Peter was even the bishop of the church at Rome at the time of his death. Tradition has it that the "Basilica of St. Peter" in Rome is built over the spot where Peter was buried. And, although the New Testament does not support a visit of Peter to Rome, there is historical evidence that he spent at least part of his later years there.

There are also numerous writings by second and third century church scholars, which confirm that Peter did die in Rome, during the reign of the Emperor Nero. The great early church scholar, Eusebius, tells us that A.D. 68 is the approximate year of his death. The early church apologists, Tertullian and Origen, both write that Peter was executed by way of crucifixion, upside down, on a cross in Rome, during the Emperor Nero's persecution of thousands of Jewish Christians, near the end of his reign. These executions are said to have occurred at the Neronian Gardens, where the estate of the Vatican is now located. According to Tertullian and Origen, Peter was buried nearby at the foot of Vatican Hill.

Almost 200 years later, it is said that Peter's remains were dug up and placed in a vault, along with the apostle Paul's, for protection against desecration, after the Emperor Valerian began his persecutions of the Christians in A.D. 258. Later, his remains were returned to the original gravesite, and circa A.D. 325, the Emperor Constantine, who was the first Christian Emperor, erected a magnificent basilica over the gravesite. This, basilica, was replaced by the present-day Saint Peter's Basilica, in the sixteenth century.

Together with James and John, (the sons of Zebedee and Salome), Peter formed the inner circle of JESUS' twelve original disciples and was constantly in the company of the SAVIOR. He is present on several notable occasions with James and John such as the raising of Jairus' daughter (Mark 5:22), the Transfiguration (Mark 9:2), and in the garden of Gethsemane, the site of JESUS' arrest on the eve of HIS crucifixion (Mark 14:32-33).

Like all of the other disciples, nothing is known of Peter's early life. We do know, however, that he was married and lived in a house in Capernaum with his brother Andrew and his mother-in-law (Mark 1:29). His occupation was that of a fisherman, and Luke's gospel tells us that he partnered in business with James and John.

Scripture also tells us that Peter was the only disciple, who, ever publicly denied JESUS, and New Testament gospel writers tell us that, he did it three times. In Matthew 26:74, Mark 14:71, Luke 22:60, and John 18:27, Peter denied JESUS for the third and final time.

It is said that a man can be a bad musician, and yet, be passionately in love with music. And I believe that for whatever Peter may have done, concerning his denial, which was brought on by fear, and no matter how terrible his failure may have been, he was passionately devoted to JESUS.

Although Peter may have been overconfident at times, as he was when he told JESUS that he would never deny HIM, it is a well-known fact, that, sometimes when a man says, "That's the one thing I will never do", oftentimes, that is the very thing that he needs to carefully guard against doing.

Satan often attacks a person at a point were they are most sure of themselves, because he knows that it is there, where they are most likely to be unprepared.
The shame of failure and disloyalty can never be a total loss, because it often lends to us a feeling of sympathy and understanding, that, otherwise, we may have never had.

"Do you love me?" is what JESUS said to Peter, as HE sought to re-instate him, following his greatest failure, which was denying his LORD and SAVIOR. And I guess, in spite of all of our failures, the only way to really prove our love for JESUS is by loving others. Love is the greatest privilege in the world, yet, it brings with it, the greatest responsibility. And we now know that, for Peter, it brought a cross, where he ultimately died for the LORD. Yes, he too, died on a cross, where Jewish tradition has it that, he requested to be nailed upside down, because he felt unworthy to die in the same manner as CHRIST JESUS.

Love always involves responsibility, and, it always involves a sacrifice. We don't really love JESUS, unless we are willing to take on HIS task, and take up our cross.
We may never be able to write, or think, like the apostle John. In fact, we may never be able to travel to the ends of the earth, and preach like the apostle Paul. But, here's where we can all follow in the footsteps of the apostle Peter. If we love JESUS, each of us can help someone else guard against going astray. If we love JESUS, each of us can love one another. And, if we love JESUS, each of us can feed Jesus' sheep, with the nourishing spiritual food, of the word of GOD.

THE APOSTLE JAMES (Son of Zebedee and Salome)

The apostle James is never mentioned apart from his brother John in the New Testament, not even in his death. But, whenever the brothers are mentioned in the gospels, James is always mentioned first. This is probably because he was the older of the two brothers.

"James" is actually the name of two of JESUS' original disciples and is also the name of several people mentioned in the New Testament, including one of JESUS' brothers. After the resurrection, however, John became the more prominent of the two brothers, and this may have been because of John's close association with the Apostle Peter. James and John, were nicknamed by JESUS, "The sons of thunder".

After JESUS had summoned Andrew and Peter, HE walked a little ways down the shore of the Sea of Galilee and summoned James and John, who were in a ship mending nets. They both immediately responded to JESUS' calling, leaving their jobs on the boat and accepting HIS invitation to follow HIM. James became "James the greater" among the group of disciples.

James' and John's mother, Salome, is believed to be a sister of Mary, the mother of JESUS, and was often known to take care of JESUS' daily needs (Mark 15:40-41 & Matthew 27:56). If this is true, then, James and John would be first cousins to JESUS. This would also help explain Salome's bold request, on behalf of her sons, that they, be given places of honor in JESUS' coming kingdom (Matthew 20:20-28).

James' greatest distinction from the other disciples is that he was the first of the twelve to die a martyr's death, when he was executed by sword, on the order of King Herod Agrippa I (Acts 12:2). He is also the only disciple whose death is actually recorded in scripture. Jewish tradition says that his death occurred in A.D. 44, when he would have been, still, quite young.

The Christian persecutions by Herod Agrippa, that involved the death of James, inspired a new fervor within the Christian movement. Agrippa had undoubtedly hoped to squash the movement altogether by executing one of its leaders. However, his plan backfired, and he, instead, caused their efforts for "The Way" of CHRIST to grow and multiply, ever the more rapidly.

James is said to have been the first Christian missionary to Spain, and, Roman Catholic authorities say that his bones are buried in the city of Santiago in northwestern Spain.

—

THE APOSTLE JOHN

We have considerably more information about the Apostle John, than we do about his brother James. In fact, we have more information on John than we do on any of the other disciples. As I told you earlier, he was the son of Zebedee and Salome, and, was a fisherman alongside his brother James and their father.

John, like his brother James, was likely born in Bethsaida. The family seemed to be pretty well off, as their father, Zebedee, employed hired servants to help, he and his sons, in their fishing business. John's call by JESUS occurred at the very same time as his brother James' and he and his brother appear throughout the synoptic gospels as fiery and zealous followers of CHRIST.

After JESUS' departure, John appears as present in Jerusalem with Peter and the other apostles. He is considered to be next to Peter in prominence, among those who bear testimony to the fact of the Transfiguration, and, the resurrection of CHRIST.

The Apostle Paul writes in Galatians 2:9 that John, along with James (the LORD's brother), and Peter, were considered pillars of the Church at Jerusalem, and were perceived in a grace that was shared with he and Barnabas, along with their right hand in fellowship. They also encouraged Paul and Barnabas to continue their teachings to the Gentiles, while they themselves focused on the Jews.

It is not clear whether John belonged to James' more conservative group at Jerusalem, or to Peter's more liberal group, and the subsequent history of John is a little bit more obscure. However, we do know, for instance, that he lived longer than all the other apostles. Polycrates, who was bishop of Ephesus, attested in A.D. 196, that, John was buried in Ephesus and was a priest who wore the gold plate, which distinguished the high-priestly mitre.

Irenaeus, another historian (A.D. 181-191), tells us that John lived up until the time of the emperor Trajan, and that he published his gospel while living in Ephesus. This account is also held by later writers such as Tertullian, who also adds that John was banished to Patmos after he had miraculously survived the punishment of being immersed in boiling hot oil.

While it is evident that legendary stories surrounding the Apostle John date back to the time of Polycrates, the real value in these accounts will forever be scrutinized by examination of their ultimate sources by scholars. Opponents of these traditions argue that there is an absence of positive evidence before the latter part of the second century, particularly in the writings of Papias, or, in the epistles of Ignatius, or of Polycarp, who was Irenaeus' mentor.

Some of these opponents assume that Iranaeus misunderstood Polycarp, which is not that hard to do. The great historian, Eusebius (circa 310-313) is compelled to point out that Papias testified of two Johns, the Apostle John, and, the presbyter John. He believes that Iranaeus is mistaken, both in identifying those two Johns, and, in holding that Papias had actually seen the apostle John. The fact that Papias, who was a companion of Polycarp, who knew the emperor Domitian, who was emperor when the Apostle John died, probably caused Iranaeus to assume that Polycarp and Papias had also actually met the Apostle John on some occasion.

In the ninth century, the chronicler, George the Monk, wrote that, on the authority of the second book of Papias, the Apostle John was killed by Jews some time circa A.D. 60-70. However, most scholars reject this assertion, while a select few accept it as correct.

Most believe that the apostle didn't even write his gospel until circa A.D. 85-95. They also believe that John came to Ephesus shortly after Paul founded the church there, and that he labored in Ephesus for many years, while also taking care of JESUS' mother, Mary. It is also widely believed that it is there, where John penned his Gospel account and his three known epistles, 1 John, 2 John, and 3 John. His book of Revelation was written while he was in exile on the Greek island of Patmos, after he received a vision from CHRIST HIMSELF.

John, like his brother James, seems to have been an impulsive young man. This would explain why soon after JESUS met them, HE nicknamed them "Sons of Thunder" (Mark 3:17). All of the Gospels mention John after his brother James, and on most occasions, it seems that James was the spokesman for the two. However, John's emotional boldness sometimes showed itself, even in front of JESUS (Mark 9:38 &). This boldness served him well at the time of JESUS' death and resurrection. In his gospel account, John 18:15, he tells us that he was known to the high priest.

Franciscan legend has it that John's family supplied fish to the high priest's household. This would have made John one of the most familiar of JESUS' followers to the high priest's guards at the time of JESUS' arrest. Nevertheless, John was the only one of the disciples bold enough to enter into the courtyards with JESUS at his first trial with the high priest, and, stand at the foot of the cross, during JESUS' crucifixion (John 19:26-27).

John's writing of the fourth gospel, his three epistles, and the book of Revelations, makes him the greatest contributor to the New Testament text, of anyone, except the Apostle Paul. It is believed that John lived to an old age and was buried in the city of Ephesus after his death.

THE APOSTLE ANDREW

Andrew, the brother of the Apostle Peter, was originally a disciple of John the Baptist. He had the honor of becoming one of the first people on earth to follow our LORD and SAVIOR, JESUS CHRIST. It was through Andrew that Peter was introduced to CHRIST (John 1:35-42), and that action by him continues to serve as a positive model for all who may be reluctant to bring their relatives to CHRIST.

The Gospel of John tells us that the day after John the Baptist saw the HOLY SPIRIT descend upon JESUS, he identified JESUS to two of his disciples. One of those men was Andrew. Intrigued by John's announcement, the two men left John's group and began to follow JESUS. John's Gospel tells us that Andrew soon went to find Peter, and through his testimony to Peter, he won him over to CHRIST.

The name "Andrew" means "manly" and implications from the Gospel writers indicate that Andrew was physically strong and was also a devout and faithful man of GOD. He was born in Bethsaida on the northern shore of Galilee. He and Peter were the sons of Jonah, a successful commercial fisherman, and they owned a house together in Capernaum (Mark 1:29). They followed their father into the fishing business.

In the Gospel of John, Andrew is mentioned only on two occasions, the feeding of the 5000 (John 6:5-9), and shortly after JESUS' entry into Jerusalem when the Greeks sought to meet and speak to JESUS (John 12:20-22). He is also mentioned a final time in the Gospel of Mark, when he asks JESUS a question concerning last things (Mark 13:3-4).

According to an account in the "Muratorian Fragment", an ancient Christian Church document that dates back to A.D. 190, Andrew served with John in Ephesus. Also the great Church historian Eusebius, says that Andrew preached in Scythia, the region north of the Black Sea, and it is for this reason that he is called the "Patron Saint of Russia". He is also considered to be the "Patron Saint of Scotland".

Other scholars mention Epirus (Gregory of Alvira), Achaea (Jerome), and Hellas (Theodoret) as places where he ministered. However, there is almost unanimous agreement that Andrew was crucified on an X-shaped cross at Patras of Achaea. The X-shaped cross has become a religious symbol of the Roman Catholic Church, and is known as the "Saint Andrew's Cross".

It is believed that Andrew was crucified on November 30, and the Roman Catholic Church, and the Greek Orthodox Church, both observe his festival annually on that date. Inspired by the memory of Andrew's missionary work in the first century, "The Order of St. Andrew", an association of church ushers who make a special effort to be courteous and kind to strangers, is still a functional ministry in those churches.

THE APOSTLE PHILIP

John's Gospel account is the only one that gives us any detailed information about the Apostle Philip. According to his gospel, Philip met JESUS at Bethany, beyond the River Jordan, where John the Baptist did most of his baptizing during his ministry. When JESUS called on Philip to be HIS disciple, he responded positively and also took JESUS and introduced HIM to his friend Nathaniel (John 1:43-51). Philip and Nathaniel, like Peter and Andrew were both, natives of the town of Bethsaida in Galilee.

Philip, whose name means, "lover of horses" was also most likely a disciple of John the Baptist, before hooking up with JESUS, shortly before John's death at the hands of Herod Antipas. Philip is mentioned on three occasions in the Gospel account the Apostle John. In two of those incidences he appears to be in close connection with the apostle Andrew, upon whom he seems to rely heavily, because of his shy and timid nature. The third incident is at the, now famous, "Last Supper" where his openhearted, enthusiastic request to be shown the FATHER gives us an indication of his naivety.

In one of only two miracles that are recorded in all four Gospels, "The feeding of the 5000", Philip had asked JESUS how they would feed the hungry crowd who had come to hear JESUS speak. Before JESUS miraculously fed the crowd, HE tested Philip's faith by asking him how he thought so many people could possibly be fed by them. Instead of responding in faith, Philip began to calculate the amount of food, and the cost it would incur (John 6:5-7).

On another occasion, when a group of Greek men came to Philip and asked him to introduce them to JESUS, a shy Philip, once again, enlists the help of Andrew, and together, they took the men to meet JESUS (John 12:20-22). These three incidences, however, only give us a terse glimpse into the personality of Philip.

Still, the Christian Church has preserved many traditions regarding Philip's later ministry and death. Some of these traditions talk of him preaching in France, while others say that he preached in southern Russia, Asia Minor, and even India.

Polycrates of Antioch, who was a bishop in Ephesus in the first century, states in his letter written to Pope Victor on the Easter controversy in A.D. 194, that, Philip was buried in Hierapolis. However, this claim cannot be otherwise substantiated, and in fact, may be a confusion with Philip the evangelist, from the book of Acts (Acts 8:4- 40), who had four daughters who were buried in Hierapolis.

THE APOSTLE MATTHEW

In the first century, the Roman government levied various taxes on the people of Palestine. The jobs of collecting taxes for transporting goods by land and sea were contracted out to private entities. Those private entities would pay a set fee to the Roman government to obtain the right to assess these taxes. These licensed entities, in turn, made their profit by charging a higher toll than the law required.

These tax collectors, or, private intities, would, more often than not, hire minor officials called "Publicans" to do the actual work of collecting the taxes directly from the people. These, Publicans, would then tack on an additional amount to the taxes in order to obtain wages for themselves.

This was the position that Matthew held at the time when JESUS called him to be a disciple. He collected taxes on the road between Damascus and Accho. His booth was located just outside of the city of Capernaum. It is believed that Matthew also collected taxes from the local fishermen based on the amount of their daily catches.

A Publican would usually charge a fee of five percent of the purchase price of trade items, and up to twelve and a half percent of the sell of a luxury item. The Jews considered the tax collector's money unclean and would never ask for their change back if they did not have the exact correct amount.

The Jewish people despised the Publicans, especially those Jews, like Matthew, who were working as agents to the Roman government, and felt that, once money touched their hands, it was no longer any good. Publicans were not even allowed to testify in court, nor, were they allowed to tithe in the temple. Matthew belonged to the class of tax collectors called "mokhsa", who were, those Jewish officials who collected taxes from travelers.

Matthew, was apparently, a well-to-do man, whose wealth was evidenced, by his being able to throw a large banquet in his home, with JESUS, as the quest of honor (Luke 5:29). The fact that he owned his own home would seem to indicate that he was wealthier than most of his fellow Publicans. He may have also been related to the disciple James, since both are said to be sons of Alphaeus (Matthew 10:3, Mark 2:14).

Matthew's name was Levi before he decided to follow JESUS. The name "Matthew" was most likely given to him by JESUS, and it means, "Gift of GOD". It may be interesting to note that, following his call by JESUS, Matthew's name is not mentioned again in the New Testament.

Even outside of the New Testament, the only statement of any importance in regard to Matthew is found in the writings of the second century scholar, Papias, which was preserved by the scholar Eusebius, and he states that, Matthew composed his oracles in the Hebrew language. We do not know what happened to Matthew after the day of Pentecost, and legend varies as to whether he died a martyr's death, or a natural death. In John Foxe's "Book of Martyrs", Foxe states that Matthew spent his last years preaching in Parthia and Ethiopia, and was martyred in the city of Nadabah in A.D. 60.

In Mark 2:13-14, we see JESUS' call for Matthew, who was a hated Tax Collector, to "follow ME". This, of course, was much to the displeasure of both the other Disciples, and the Pharisees. Being a Tax Collector, Matthew was one of the most hated men in town. But JESUS always wants the man, that, no one else wants.

Of all of the Disciples, Matthew probably gave up the most. When he left his Tax Collector job that day, he automatically burned his bridges with the Roman government. There could be no return to such a position of trust in the Roman government, by a Jewish citizen. He had made a decision that would cut him off from all that he had known in life, however, the person who has contempt, or fear in his heart, can never be a "fisher of men" any way.

Charles T. Studs, the great twentieth century missionary for CHRIST, had a favorite quote that he always loved to use. He would oftentimes say that, "Some people want to live within the sound of the Church, or Chapel bell, I want to run a rescue shop for souls, within a yard of Hell".

The miracle of JESUS' forgiveness transformed Matthew from being one of the most hated men in town, into the author of, perhaps, the most important book, the world will ever read. When Matthew left his Tax Collector's table that day, he gave up much in the material sense, but in the spiritual sense, he became heir to a fortune.

———

THE APOSTLE THOMAS

The Apostle John's gospel gives us a lot more information on the apostle Thomas than does the synoptic gospels of Matthew, Mark, and Luke. John tells us that Thomas was also called "Didymus" (John 20:4), which is the Greek word for "twins". The word "thom" in the Hebrew language also means "twin". Jerome's "Latin Vulgate", which is the first Latin translation of the Holy Bible, uses the name, Didymus, as his proper name, and, most English versions of scripture followed suit until the beginning of the twentieth century.

Scripture does not tell us anything about Thomas' life before he was called to join JESUS' original disciples, nor does it tell us anything about his family background. However, his joining the six other disciples who returned to the fishing boats after JESUS' crucifixion suggests that he too may have been a fisherman in his prior life (John 21:1-3).

Because of Thomas' well-known incident of "doubting" in John 20:25, we often forget the act of courage he displayed in John 11:16, where he shows his willingness to go to Jerusalem and die with JESUS. His inability to believe in that later incident earned him the nickname "Doubting Thomas". However, even the early church fathers respected the biblical examples of Thomas. The great church historian, Augustine, once said of Thomas, "He doubted so that we, ourselves, might not doubt".

Thomas appears three other times in the gospel of John, and except for the listing of the disciples, he does not appear in the other three gospels. On one occasion, Thomas asked JESUS, "LORD, we do not know where you are going, and how can we know the way?" (John 14:5). It is to that question that JESUS gave us HIS, now famous, response "I AM the WAY, the TRUTH, and the LIFE" (John 14:6), the sixth of HIS seven great "I AM statements" that are found in the gospel of John.

Following JESUS' resurrection, Thomas was on the Sea of Galilee with six other disciples when JESUS signaled to them from the shore and instructed them where to cast their nets (John 21:2). He was also present with the other disciples in the upper room after JESUS' ascension back into Heaven.

According to Jewish tradition, Thomas went on to preach the gospel in Parthia and Persia, where he is said to have died. However, later tradition tells us that Thomas was martyred in India. "Christians of St. Thomas" is a name often applied to the ancient Christian churches of southern India, and according to tradition, Thomas founded the Christian churches in Malabar, on the southwest coast of India, and then crossed over to Mylapur, now a suburb of Madras, where the shrine of his martyrdom is located. The shrine was rebuilt by the Portuguese in 1547, and still stands on Mount St. Thomas, where a cross is shown with a Pahlavi inscription which may be as old as the seventh century.

———

THE APOSTLE BARTHOLOMEW (Nathanael)

From the New Testament, we know nothing specifically about Bartholomew except his selection by JESUS to the apostolate. Like Thomas, he is mentioned only in the list of apostles in the synoptic gospels, and even John's gospel doesn't give us much more to go on. The synoptic gospels all agree that his name is Bartholomew, however, John's gospel lists his name as Nathanael. Some scholars believe that Bartholomew was the surname of Nathanael.

The name "Bartholomew" means "son of Talmai", in the Aramaic language, however, the scriptures do not identify who Talmai is. He may have been named after King Talmai of Geshur who is mentioned in 2 Samuel 3:3. Some scholars believe Bartholomew was connected with the Ptolemies, who were the ruling family of Egypt. This theory is based on a statement by Jerome that Bartholomew was the only apostle of noble birth.

According to Church tradition, Bartholomew was a missionary to various countries, such as India and Armenia, where he preached along side Thomas and Philip. The manner of his death is unclear as one tradition has it that he was beheaded, while another has him dying a horrible death, as he was skinned alive and then crucified upside down.

The latter tradition is said to be what inspired Michelangelo to portray Nathanael in one of his paintings holding his own skin in his hands. The Venerable Bede said that Nathanael was skinned alive and then beheaded by King Astriagis in India after he had declared war on all Christians in A.D. 62.

———

THE APOSTLE JAMES (Son of Alpheus)

The Gospels make only fleeting references to this James, who was the son of Alpheus, and, most likely, the brother of the apostle Matthew. Scripture tells us that Matthew's father was also named Alpheus. Most scholars believe that this James is also the same as the "James the less" (James the younger) mentioned in Mark 15:40 as being the son of a lady named Mary, who sat and watched JESUS' crucifixion from a distance, along with Mary Magdelene and Salome. If this Apostle James was the same as the "James the less" mentioned in Mark 15:40, he would have also been a cousin of JESUS.

Some bible scholars theorize that this disciple James bore a close physical resemblance to JESUS. This could explain why Judas Iscariot had to identify JESUS with a kiss, to the group that came to arrest HIM in the Garden of Gethsemane, on the night of JESUS' betrayal (Mark 14:43-45 & Luke 22:47-48). It is said that James went on to preach in Persia, where he was eventually crucified. However, there is no concrete proof concerning his later ministry and death.

———

THE APOSTLE JUDAS (not Iscariot)

In John 14:22, the Apostle John refers to one of the disciples as "Judas, not Iscariot". It is that Judas of whom I refer to here. The Apostle John was careful, as he sought to avoid any confusion with Judas Iscariot, the traitor. It is this Judas, whom Jerome, the author of the Vulgate, dubbed as "Trionius", which means, "the man with three names".

The Apostle Matthew calls this Judas "Lebbeus", whose surname was "Thaddeus" (Matthew 10:3). Mark simply refers to him as "Thaddeus" in his gospel account (Mark 3:18), while Luke refers to him as "Judas the son of James" (Luke 6:16 & Acts 1:13).

The King James Version incorrectly translates Luke as saying that Judas was the brother of James. William Steuart McBirnie suggests that the name "Thaddeus" is a diminutive form of "Theudas", which comes from the Aramaic noun "Tad", meaning "breast". Therefore, the name Thaddeus was probably a nickname that literally meant "one close to the breast", or "one beloved". As for the name "Lebbeus", it is probably derived from the Hebrew noun "Leb", which means "heart".

The great Church historian, Eusebius, wrote that JESUS once sent Judas to King Abgar of Mesopotamia to pray for his healing. According to this story, after JESUS' ascension back into Heaven, Judas went to King Abgar and remained in Mesopotamia and preached in several cities there. It is said, according to one tradition, that Judas was slain by a group of magicians in the city of Suanir of Persia with clubs and stones. Judas is also said to have preached the gospel in Syria and Arabia, and to have suffered martyrdom while in Syria.

———

THE APOSTLE SIMON (Zelotes)

The Scriptures do not indicate when Simon was invited to join JESUS' original group of disciples, however, tradition says that JESUS called him at around the same time he called Andrew, Peter, James, John, Judas Iscariot, and Thaddeus.

Simon, "the Canaanaean" is found in the lists of Matthew and Mark, and is identified as the same person as Simon Zelotes. The epithet "Canaanean" is a reproduction of the Aramaic word for "Zealot".

Luke gives us the Greek translation "Zelotes", however, there is no real need to think that Simon was a member of the party of "Zealots" or "Nationalists" who waged bitter opposition against the Roman Empire in the first century. The name can also simply denote one's zealousness for the law.

The later history of Simon's life is very obscure, as much legend is connected with him. One of those legends connects him as one of the brothers of JESUS, who succeeded James as bishop of Jerusalem, however, this is not likely. It is also said that this Simon preached in Persia, and, in Egypt, something that may be highly probable.

The Coptic Church of Egypt says that Simon did indeed preach in Egypt, Great Britain, and Persia. Nicephorus of Constantinople wrote that;

"Simon who was born in Cana of Galilee and was surnamed Zelotes, having received the HOLY GHOST from above, traveled through Egypt and Africa, and then, through Mauretania and Libya, preaching the Gospel. And the same doctrine he taught to the Occidental Sea and the Isles called Britanniae".

———

THE APOSTLE PAUL

The Apostle Paul was the first great Christian missionary and theologian, after the example of CHRIST JESUS. Born and raised under the strictest of Jewish tradition and Judaism, Paul went on to become the first to clearly distinguish between Judaism and the Gospel of CHRIST JESUS. He presented Christianity as the universal religion for all mankind, and not just for a tiny sect of Judaism for the benefit of the Jews.

During his time, Paul became widely known as the apostle of the Gentiles. He solved, once and for all, the issues that arose, between the problems people had with Christianity, and the biblical and non-biblical traditions of the Jewish law. While the other apostles continued on with a practical attitude toward the Law and Judaism, oftentimes, not seeing far into principles, Paul, on the other hand, preached that the issue was very much different than Judaism, and that the doctrine of CHRIST, that he preached, was defined by the cross. He felt that one either had to choose "Pharisaism", or "JESUS", or quite literally, "Law", or "Love", as the ultimate revelation of GOD.

Paul (Saul) was born and raised in Tarsus of Cilicia, as Gaius Julius Paulus, and was the son of a Roman citizen. Much of what has been written about Paul would probably never have been written, if Luke had mentioned his full name. This is mainly because our view of him would have likely, then, been transformed. The view by others, of his Tarsian citizenship, would have probably, too greatly influenced the thinking of first-century readership.

All of Paul's letters bear traces of the Hellenistic culture of which he was raised, and he certainly obtained many of his Greek ideas through the medium of Judaeo-Greek, or, Hellenistic literature. A careful study of his letters gives us some idea of this societal element in his early life, due to his Jewish birth. They suggest Paul's own youthful attitude toward the importance and responsibility of being born Jewish.

Paul was a Pharisee, and the son of a Pharisee (Acts 23:6), and so, we can be certain that his religious training found its roots in loyalty to the regulations of the Law, as it was interpreted by the Jewish rabbis. At the age of 13 he was expected to assume personal responsibility for his obedience to the Law.

As a rabbinic student, Paul was required to learn a trade so that he would not be a burden to the people, once he assumed his role as a teacher. He proved to be an apt student, as he flourished in his enthusiasm for ancestral traditions, and, in his zeal for the Jewish law.

Much is known about how Paul came to believe in the person and works of CHRIST JESUS and other matters crucial to the Christian faith. His letters are forever preserved in the pages of the New Testament, as they bear eloquent testimony to the passion of his conviction, and strength of his logic. Throughout each of his biblical letters we see bits and pieces of his own autobiography, and we also find a broad outline of his activities chronicled in Luke's Book of the Acts of the Apostles.

Paul was a tremendously persuasive preacher and his boyhood studies under the great first-century scholar Gamaliel had strengthened greatly, his Hebrew orthodoxy. After completing his studies under Gamaliel at the school of Hillel, Paul probably returned to Tarsus for a few years.

No clear evidence exists that tells us rather or not he ever encountered JESUS during JESUS' earthly ministry in the flesh. However, after being re-directed by JESUS that day on the road to Damascus, Paul began to point to his own life and work as proof of his message. He heralded his own personal experience and he exhorted his listeners to believe in the good news of CHRIST JESUS, our SAVIOR.

According to Paul's own writings, and, from the writings of Luke in the Book of Acts, we know that Paul returned to Jerusalem where he dedicated a great deal of his energies to the persecution of the Jews who had accepted the teachings of JESUS, through HIS disciples, and other "Adherents of the Way of CHRIST". His zeal for the Jewish laws found a ready outlet in his assault on the Christian Church at Jerusalem during its infancy. For Paul, the Christian Church presented a threat to all that he held dear, in regards to his strict Jewish upbringing.

Paul's autobiographical reference contained in his first letter to his young friend Timothy (1 Timothy 1:13-15), goes a long way into shedding some light as to why a sensitive man, such as Paul, could ever have become involved in such violence against his own people. There Paul states that even though he once blasphemed and persecuted CHRIST and HIS people, he received mercy from GOD for his ignorant behavior. Paul goes on to state that he was "the foremost of all sinners".

Stephen, the first martyr of the Christian Church, after the example of CHRIST, was one of the most outspoken leaders of the new Christian movement. In Acts chapter 7, we see Luke's chronicles of how Paul publicly associated himself with the "Libertines" who executed Stephen. He then went on an aggressive campaign to suppress and devastate the Christian Church at Jerusalem, going from house to house dragging men and women out and throwing them in jail.

Three years after Paul's conversion to the Christian Movement, he left Damascus and went to Jerusalem, where he first became acquainted with the Apostle Peter, and James, the brother of JESUS, through Barnabas (Acts 9:27-28) (Galatians 1:18-19). However, because of the animosity of his former associates, he had to leave Jerusalem under duress, and was taken by those who helped him escape, down to Caesarea, and from there, he was put on a ship back to his hometown of Tarsus, where he remained for nine years.

Not many details of that period in Paul's life are known. However, at the end of that time, Barnabas went down to Tarsus and brought him back to Antioch of Syria to help him with the new Christian Church that had been started up there (Acts 11:25 26). It was there in Antioch of Syria, a predominately Gentile city, that the term "Christian" was first used. The church at Antioch went on to become the "missionary headquarters" of the early Christian Movement.

After about a year, and, because of the success that Paul and Barnabas were having in the conversion of Gentiles in Antioch, both men, where commissioned by the Church at Jerusalem, to concentrate their efforts on evangelizing, and taking the Gospel of CHRIST to Gentiles everywhere. The way was now open for the onset of

Paul and Barnabas' first and only missionary journey together. Before the beginning of their second journey, however, they fell out over differences involving John Mark, Barnabas' cousin, and the eventual author of the Book of Mark. Paul had been disappointed with John Mark because he had abandoned them during their first mission while in Pamphylia (Acts 13:13).

For his second missionary journey, Paul chose Silas to partner with him, while Barnabas and John Mark teamed up and left to begin their mission on the island of Cyprus, Barnabas' birthplace, and the rest is history. Scripture records that Paul went on to do a third missionary journey, however, it does say whether or not Barnabas did the same.

Paul is the only New Testament writer who refers to the Christian Church as a "Body". He suggests that each member of the church is interdependent on one another, not unlike the parts of our human body. Each part works in harmony with the other for the good of the whole body, just as the parts of the human body functions best when all the parts follow the direction of the head. The "human body", and, the "Church body", functions best, when they commit and submit themselves to the direction and leadership of CHRIST JESUS.

To give full justice to "Paulinism" in any respect, we must compare it with other interpretations of CHRIST JESUS and HIS Gospel in the time immediately following JESUS' ascension back into Heaven. At one end of the spectrum we find "Judaeo-Christianity", with all of its ultra-conservatism and undeveloped spirituality; and on the other end, we see "Gnosticism", with its heaping dose of ultra-spiritualism, arising out of a very rigid dualism, and a defective sense of historical continuity in its revelation.

Somewhere in between these two extremes, we find the Apostle Paul, perhaps, blending the ideals of both into a religious unity of immense ethical power and initiative. And while many have discovered themselves in the writings of Paul, and felt his religious appeal, more than a few others have misunderstood the theoretic setting of his message.

In the final verses of the book of Acts, while under house arrest, Paul met in Rome with several enthusiastic representatives of the Christian church there. He wanted to meet with them out of a deep compassion and concern for them as Jewish brothers, and, for their GOD-given right to hear the Gospel first among the people of the world. His presentation that day won little response however, but as a result of that meeting, Paul felt released to concentrate even more on his ministry to the Gentiles.

Church history tells us that Paul was soon acquitted of the bogus charges against him and he left Rome and continued to minister for about three years in other

Gentile settings. However, upon his return to Rome, he was re-arrested, and shortly afterwards, was executed, probably by decapitation, near the end of the reign of the Emperor Nero in the mid-60's A.D.

CLOSING REMARKS

The four pillars of any good and sound relationship are love, trust, respect, and understanding. All four must exist in our relationship with GOD, and, they must also exist in our relationships with each other.

Whoever wrote this wonderful Book of Hebrews felt a need to reassure the Jewish believers that their faith in CHRIST JESUS as the MESSIAH was sound and reasonable. They already possessed three of the four pillars necessary for a sound relationship with CHRIST, love, trust, and respect, and now, he wanted to instill the fourth element, which is, understanding.

In Luke 24:44-49, after JESUS had proven to HIS disciples that HE had really risen and was not a ghost, HE begins to show them all of the various written facts from the Old Testament regarding HIMSELF as the MESSIAH. HE opened up their minds to understand and receive these scriptures from Moses and the prophets, and, the Psalms. HE made them to understand how the MESSIAH was to suffer and die, and then, rise again from the dead on the third day. Here, we can see that, the efforts of this writer of Hebrews, is no different than those of CHRIST before him.

GOD had long ago promised to Abraham that he would be the father of HIS chosen nation of people, and long ago, HE had delivered that promise. HE promised David a kingdom that would last forever, and through CHRIST JESUS, HE had delivered that promise also. In Luke 24:49, JESUS left HIS troubled-hearted followers with the re-iteration of the promise of the HOLY SPIRIT, WHO would come to comfort, counsel, and guide mankind along the path of righteousness for the remainder of our time, here on earth.

Easter is the time of the year when the death, burial, and resurrection of our LORD and SAVIOR JESUS CHRIST is at the forefront of the minds of most professed Christians. "This do in remembrance of ME" is what JESUS said to HIS disciples. However, it is also a statement that comes to us, from across the spans of times, in hopes that we too, can share in this New Covenant promise of salvation.

JESUS knew how quickly the human mind would forget. HE knew that we would become so pre-occupied with our own worldly affairs, that, eventually, we would fail to recall HIS OWN vicarious sacrifice. And so, HE invites us to come in sometimes, into the peace and tranquility of HIS FATHER's house, and to do this, in remembrance of HIM. If, in HIS house, we pledge ourselves to HIM, and then go out and fail to reflect HIS image to others, through our behavior, then, we too, like Judas Iscariot, have become traitors to HIS cause.

Unlike JESUS, we don't know when our last supper will be. It is the will of GOD that man not know what HIS time, place, or method of demise will be. However, like

JESUS, we can, all become great Preparers, and begin to store up our treasures in a place, that, JESUS says, has been prepared for us, from the very foundation of this world. That place that Luke, Paul, and other New Testament writers call, in the Greek, "paradeisos" (par-ad-i-sos), but we call, "The Kingdom of Heaven".

The author of the Book of Hebrews exalts and acknowledges JESUS as the divine culmination of GOD's revelation through the Old Testament prophets. This divine revelation that is personified in CHRIST is superior in every respect.

Larry D. Alexander

THE GREAT COMMISSION

And JESUS came and spake unto them, saying, "All power is given unto me in Heaven and in Earth. Go ye therefore, and teach all nations, baptizing them in the name of the FATHER, and of the SON, and of the HOLY GHOST: Teaching them to observe all things whatsoever I have commanded you: and, lo, I am with you always, even unto the end of the world". Amen. - Matthew 28:18-20

–

THE ROMANS ROAD TO SALVATION:

The first and foremost duty of the Christian is to lead people to CHRIST and present them with an opportunity to accept HIS gift of Salvation, first with their lips, so that they may later come to accept HIM in their hearts, through the study of GOD's word, and, through the power and guidance of the HOLY SPIRIT. The following exercise is incorporated in this book to enable you to do just that, and is known to serious Christians, quite simply, as the "Romans Road to Salvation".

(1). Start by letting the person you're leading, know that all mankind is on the same level, as far as who is good, and who is not.

WHO IS GOOD?

"As it is written, There is none righteous, no, not one:" – ROMANS 3:10

–

(2). Let them know that, clearly, we have sinned and the bible confirms it.

WHO HAS SINNED?

"For all have sinned, and come short of the glory of GOD;" - ROMANS 3:23

–

(3). Tell them where sin came from.

WHERE DID SIN COME FROM?

"Wherefore, as by one man sin entered into the world, and death by sin; and so death passed upon all men, for that all have sinned:" - ROMANS 5:12

—

(4). Tell them what sin costs us.

GOD'S PRICE ON SIN

"For the wages of sin is death; but the gift of GOD is eternal life through JESUS CHRIST our LORD." – ROMANS 6:23

—

(5). Let them know that the price of sin is paid.

WHO PAID THE PRICE?

"But GOD commendeth HIS love toward us, in that, while we were yet sinners, CHRIST died for us." – ROMANS 5:8

—

(6). Show them the only way out.

THE ONLY WAY OUT

"That if thou shalt confess with thy mouth the LORD JESUS, and shalt believe in thine heart that GOD hath raised HIM from the dead, thou shalt be saved. For with the heart man believeth unto righteousness; and with the mouth confession is made unto Salvation" – ROMANS 10:9-10

—

(7). If they now wish to give their life to CHRIST, have them repeat after you, this prayer, or a similarly effective prayer.

LORD JESUS, I need YOU.

I thank YOU for dying on the cross for my sins.
I do earnestly repent for my trespasses against YOU,
And I open up the door to my heart,
And invite YOU in, as my LORD and SAVIOR.
I thank YOU for forgiving my sins,
And then offering me Eternal Life.
I accept YOUR offer of Salvation,
And I want YOU to take control of the throne of my life,
And make me into the kind of person that YOU want me to be.
It is in YOUR precious name that I pray. Amen.

I urge you to become familiar with this application, as it is the most important lesson in this book. If a Christian does not know how to bring another person to CHRIST, he or she is not a complete Christian. If a Christian knows this application, and yet, does not use it to save others, GOD will not hold you blameless for your fellowman's demise. Take heed and keep yourself in the love of GOD.
Amen.

www.ingramcontent.com/pod-product-compliance
Lightning Source LLC
Chambersburg PA
CBHW081154090426
42736CB00017B/3317